No DATA FOR FILES OR RESEARCH
GOOD BOOK ON EXPERIENCES OF A
        MORTAR OBSERVER IN EUROPE
128-130 SOUND OF NEBELWERFERS.

THE LAST KILOMETER

An Association of the U.S. Army Book

A. PRESTON PRICE

THE LAST KILOMETER

Marching to Victory in Europe
with the Big Red One, 1944–1945

NAVAL INSTITUTE PRESS ☆ ANNAPOLIS, MARYLAND

Naval Institute Press
291 Wood Road
Annapolis, MD 21402

Library of Congress Cataloging-in-Publication Data
Price, A. Preston, 1921-
    The last kilometer : marching to victory in Europe with the
Big Red One, 1944-1945 / A. Preston Price.
    p. cm.
    Includes index.
    ISBN 1-55750-434-2 (alk. paper)
    1. Price, A. Preston, 1921- 2. World War, 1939-1945—Campaigns—
Western Front. 3. World War, 1939-1945—Personal narratives,
American. 4. United States. Army. Infantry Division, 1st—Biography.
5. United States. Army—Officers—Biography. I. Title.
    D811.P655 A3 2002
    940.54'1273—dc21

                                                    2001044876

Printed in the United States of America on acid-free paper ∞
09 08 07 06 05 04 03 02   9 8 7 6 5 4 3 2
First printing

CONTENTS

Acknowledgments   vii

1   To Europe   1

2   To the Front   8

3   Holding the Corner   17

4   The Attack   39

5   Waiting on the River   74

6   Roer to the Rhine   86

7   Remagen Bridgehead   116

8   The Rose Pocket   149

9   The Harz Mountains   163

10   Into Czechoslovakia   185

Index   197

ACKNOWLEDGMENTS

My thanks to my dear wife, Alice Louise Stevenson Price, without whom we never would have brought this story to fruition, and to my sons—Stevenson Hickham Price, my computer expert and lawyer son, who makes all things possible; Col. Richard Preston Price (Ret.), my engineer son, who provided the original map of the 26th Infantry's route; and Douglas Sterling Price, my physician son, for his caring attitude and support. Also, many thanks to the U.S. Army McCormick Research Center of the First Division Museum at Cantigny in Wheaton, Illinois, for the photos they provided for this work.

THE LAST KILOMETER

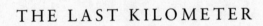

Lieutenant Price's and the
26th Infantry's Route Across Europe

1 ☆

TO EUROPE

It is late in November 1944, the twenty-first to be exact, and I am sailing from New York Harbor aboard the SS *China Mail*. I am one of twenty replacement officers, all second lieutenants, headed for the European theater of operations, or ETO. We are lucky in that we are not crossing on one of the large troopships but riding the "gravy train" in the form of a new and fast diesel cargo ship. There are few restrictions aboard ship, and knowing that we will soon be in combat, I hasten to drink in all of the beauty an ocean voyage can bring.

Most of the voyage I spend on the decks, and though the weather is bad, and most of the other officers take to their bunks, or the rails, with various states of seasickness, I find that, as in the past, I do not succumb to that horrid ailment of the sea. Instead, I spend my time alone, sitting on the poop deck, reading with immense delight, and resting my eyes by staring out across the water, swirling and turbulent where the ship's propeller disturbs it, to the other ships in the mighty convoy, or looking in the opposite direction at the horizon, broken with the irregularities of the waves. On stormy days, I take a curious delight in standing at the very bow of the ship as it plunges up and down, feeling the wind tear at my hair, watching the bow sink deeper and deeper into the green froth until it finally drives me from my perch with the tremendous floods of water that pour over it. No drenching can dismay me, for this is the life. Why worry about the future when here all around me is the immensity of the present, the mystery of the sea?

All too quickly the trip ends, on December fourth, and we make landfall off the port rail—Ireland. I watch the distant, misty outline of that country with mixed emotions. Here, in the midst of all this turmoil, with the whole world threatened by an arrogant people, is a land that seems to take no heed of the millions suffering. But such thoughts soon leave my mind as I realize that tomorrow I will be on land again, in Europe. I must confess that I am greatly worried, and the uncertain future holds a not-too-rosy picture for me. As an infantryman, I am aware that soon I will be in the bitterest part of the war. Altogether too soon I will find out the sort of stuff of which I am made.

It is interesting to note the various attitudes among the lieutenants as we near Europe. Some of them are quiet, and worried; in fact, one almost has a nervous breakdown. On the other hand, there are a few who brag loudly of what they are going to do, and the usual lot who have a soft job "all lined up." None of that combat stuff for them. I do not know how I appear to the other lieutenants, for though I have always been able to analyze the personalities of others, I am unable to analyze myself. I become absorbed in studying my shipmates and draw many conclusions about them at the daily German classes I give during the voyage.

I think these classes in the fundamentals of German are

good indications of the state of mind one falls into on a sea voyage. Knowing that I will have a hard time occupying myself, on the third day out I offer to teach some simple German to the officers. At first there are only a few takers, but as the second day rolls around, I find my class growing, and soon all but a few of the diehards are hard at work on *ich bin, du bist, er ist*. Toward the end of the trip, attendance drops. As the soldiers become increasingly occupied with their own worries, many find the language routine galling and tiresome.

A lieutenant who came aboard the ship when we landed in Wales tells us some of the most unadulterated tripe about combat, morals, and the value of a bottle of liquor in the ETO. This from a man who probably has never been any nearer to combat than a western port in England. Then there is the chap who takes us off the boat. Apparently he has but one duty in life, one sole, single purpose for existence. He is to take us to a train, put us on the train, and see that we get started for the Southampton port of embarkation. He succeeds in the first two tasks magnificently; in the third, he fails rather miserably. The train in which we find ourselves can take us to almost any point in southern England except Southampton. At dawn, and through the courtesy of many agencies, we are at last at the Port of Southampton. We stare with all the curiosity of the novice at the signs of the bombing raids that have laid waste to most of the city.

Impressed as we are, we still have no idea of the holocaust of war, because most of Southampton's damage has been cleaned up. Where formerly stood three blocks of houses, now there is only a field, and none of us can imagine what the three blocks looked like, say, ten minutes after the raid. Yes, we have a lot to see, and a lot to learn. We are taken to a tent city that has been set up in one of Southampton's loveliest parks, and there we sit shivering for one day. By this time all of us are moody and quiet.

The next morning, December sixth, we march about three miles to a pier, and there we board a channel steamer manned by a British crew. We are all greatly impressed by the sloppiness of the kitchen, and, indeed, the mutton-stench in the galley is nauseating. There is a great deal of speculation as to our final destination, but we are pretty sure that we will land near the site of the invasion. We are told that submarines and floating mines are a serious threat, and as usual we are outfitted with life jackets—this time the English type that one inflates by blowing into it. Also we are issued hammocks, which delights me, as I spent much time in a hammock when I was in the Philippines and know that there is no better way to endure a choppy sea.

I laugh watching some of the attempts to mount the hammocks. Many of the chaps pile luggage up beside the hammock, then carefully place one foot dead in the center of the canvas. When they throw their weight on that foot—well, there can be only one result when one movable object is pushed by another. All of the officers are placed on two-hour guard shifts in the various troop quarters in the ship. It is our duty, I suppose, to be there with the men so that if we are struck by a torpedo or happen to nudge a floating mine, we will drown in a military manner, because it is an awfully long way up to the deck.

We sail the following night, and on the following day, the eighth, late in the afternoon, we make out the coastline of France. I can imagine how some of the Normandy invasion troops felt on first viewing the low coastline in the distance. I am very thankful the ground we are to land on has already been captured. It is dark when we are told that this is the harbor of Le Havre we are approaching, and in the light of some floodlights on the shore we begin to see signs of a more recent conflict. We can barely discern the outlines of buildings, torn and gutted, with a black background that seems to hold all evil in store for us. This is France.

There are no harbor facilities left at Le Havre, so a landing craft puts out from the beach and heads toward us. As it comes nearer, we see that there is a problem, for the craft seems ten stories below us when it comes alongside our ship. But in no time at all the British sailors rig a gangway down to the barge and a slide affair to slide the baggage down. Then begins the long and tedious unloading. For four hours, men pour off the ship, one at a time, down, down, down. Finally, when it seems that there is no more room, it is our turn, and then I begin to work my way down the lurching steps. About halfway down we hear a tremendous splash in the water between the two ships, and the cry goes up that one of the footlockers has slipped from the slide. I am sure that each of the officers feel, as I do, that his footlocker is now at the bottom of Le Havre Harbor. We have to wait until the landing craft comes ashore to find out whose locker has fallen.

The beaching of a landing craft is a very weird and mysterious thing. Our beaching is out of this world. As we near the shore, a sarcastic American, standing on the tiny deck of the vessel, gives the packed throng below instructions. "We gotta take this goddamned thing at full speed," he shouts. "If we don't go in at full speed, you'll hafta swim ashore. So hang on, damn it, and brace yerselves for a shock. Now watch it, watch it!" We cling to each other for dear life and spread our legs about two yards. After waiting an interminable time, we hear the bottom touch ground, and without the slightest shock the vessel comes to a graceful stop. Rather sheepishly we look for our baggage while the curses of the king of the bridge assault our ears. "Jesus Christ, hurry up! I gotta get this craft outta here. The tide's goin' out. Hurry up, or I'll be beached all night! God damn it, shake it up!"

With a great feeling of relief I discover that my footlocker is still among those present, and by carrying several heavy loads, and with much cooperation, we get our possessions up on the rocky beach. No sooner has the last soldier left the craft than, true to his word, the skipper swings the bow gate up and backs off the beach. We pile our gear onto trucks and ride through the dead city. There seems to be no life; just street after street of jumbled junk, rubbled masonry, and stones.

We finally pass over the moat of a fort high above the city and though a sally port. Inside we unload and are told to go to a big barracks building, looming black and foreboding. Someone turns on a flashlight, and there are immediate cries of "Turn off that damned light!" and "What d'ya want to do, get us bombed?" After exploring the building from top to bottom, we spread our bedding rolls on the floors of the barracks and, by huddling close to one another, manage to sleep in the miserable cold of a building from which every window has been blasted.

The next morning we are awakened by someone running breathlessly into our rooms, saying, "Say, I forgot to tell you men last night that nobody has been in this building. It hasn't been cleared and there are probably booby traps all over the place!" When dawn comes, and with it a small portion of sunlight, we look around with a great deal of interest. The first thing we do is warily find tar paper and boards to patch up our windows in an effort to keep warm. Then in due time comes the trick I will see so often during the war. Those who are just too cold to stand it any longer decide to build a fire. They find any type of metal container and proceed to burn anything inflammable. In such cases there is only one thing to do: throw open the windows and doors and come back in about two hours, when most of the smoke has left the building.

During the day we find out many things. We are staying in Fort Ste. Addresse, which a few days earlier was occupied by the Germans. There was quite a fight for it; all of the barracks are riddled with bullet holes and shell fragments. German and British equipment is strewn about, and there are German artillery and antiaircraft pieces standing on the parapet surrounding the fort. In the afternoon a group of us walk through the town and speculate on the length of our stay. We also wonder at the cold and hostile attitude of the people of Le Havre. We later learn that it was necessary for our forces to bomb the city heavily during its occupation by the Germans and again during the invasion. To top things off, it was bombarded by units of the Atlantic Fleet when the British captured the city from the rear.

The next morning, after we decide we will be here for about one month, we suddenly are told to pack and be ready to leave in fifteen minutes.

2

TO THE FRONT

As we climb onto the trucks, I notice that each vehicle has a large red ball painted on its side. I soon find out from the driver the story of the truckers who made history. With no ports and no rail lines operating on the Continent, the thin artery that fed supplies to the rapidly advancing Allies in the fall of 1944 was the Red Ball Highway, and the trucks that carried supplies from the beaches of Normandy to the front were called "red balls." But all of this is of minor interest as we suffer through a day of riding in the back of a truck in a drizzle of rain going east across the top of France.

We reach our destination, Givet, on the border with Belgium, and are unloaded in front of an ancient soap factory that is to be home for the next few days. (Several years after the war I read an account of a British sailor who was imprisoned in Givet during the Napoleonic Wars, and from his description, I would say that the town had not changed much in the intervening 130 years.) We are taken into the factory's interior and assigned to portions of the factory. I find myself with a steel cot that has one-inch steel slats crisscrossing the frame but no mattress. The cold is intense inside the building, and there are no lights except in the portion of the building where the kitchen is located.

When one is part of a replacement stream, the constant question is, Where am I going next? Givet is no exception. All replacement depots are a hurry-up-and-wait proposition. We hurry the next day to a nearby field, where we are given ammunition and allowed to zero our weapons. I discover that the carbine I carried across the ocean is firing well and feel that I am ready to move on to the front.

I am given a platoon of replacements to command temporarily. Things, however, do not move so rapidly, and days pass with nothing to do. My nights are a little more interesting as I discover a small Belgian café doing business just about a mile away from Givet and make it my habit to patronize this establishment the next few evenings. I meet several officers whom I ply with questions about combat. I can divide them into two types: those who try to alarm the young replacement and those who try to reassure him. My chief occupation is drinking a rather watery Cognac bottled locally and sold for exorbitant prices. However, I am already suffering from that strange wartime feeling that makes money appear to have absolutely no value and do not regret the expense. I find the Belgian Cognac strangely to my liking.

Perhaps most memorable are my nightly walks back across the Belgian border to Givet. These are crisp, cold nights with beautiful star arrays, and the frozen ground crunches satisfyingly under my combat boots. I suppose that my youth, the pleasing solitude, and the Cognac combine to make these walks so enjoyable.

Suddenly everyone is talking about a German breakthrough in Belgium. The Belgian and French citizens I meet have terror written in their eyes. "Are the Bosche returning? What shall we do?" It is hard for me to fully understand the panic engendered

by the reports. These people were relieved of the German occupation just a few short weeks ago. The scars of the battle for Givet
are fresh in view; a German tank, its turret a smoke-scarred mass,
stands at the main road into Givet. The shell holes in the fields
are still fresh; rain has not softened their jagged rims.

After a day of rumors and alarm, the first survivors of the
breakthrough begin to stream into town. It is hard to grasp that
these are our soldiers. Dirty, unshaven, almost hysterical. The first
we see are from rear-echelon units that were ordered to move to
the rear but soon became combat units and fragments of units.
Just as I complete an inspection of my platoon of replacements
inside the fence of the soap factory, an engineer unit de-trucks in
front of the factory. The engineers come in, bitterness and fear
on their countenances. The officer in charge of the unit comes
straight to the front of my platoon. He ignores my salute and
addresses himself directly to my men. "Kill them!" he says. Then,
seeming to notice me for the first time, he turns to me. He appears
to be on the verge of tears as he says, "Kill them, Lieutenant. Don't
take any prisoners. Don't take any prisoners!"

In a matter of hours we are loading onto trucks. Ammunition
has been issued, and every man is ready to give a good account of
himself. Rumors of German paratroop landings sweep the town,
and we continually hear reports of German tanks reaching the
outskirts of Givet. The German penetration will, in fact, reach a
point only eight miles from Givet. To reach this point, at the height
of the breakthrough on December twenty-fourth, the German
Fifth Panzer Army will advance fifty-five miles. My truck pulls
out of Givet on the twenty-third.

This is to be my first of many combat rides. The small convoy in which we travel follows the Meuse River north to Namur,
Belgium, and then through the province of Liège. We are halted
every few miles at road blocks and checked by troops who suspect

that we are part of an enemy column. There are numerous traffic snarls, and all sorts of orders and instructions are passed on to us during our innumerable stops: "If we are strafed, we won't stop. We'll keep going. If the paratroopers catch the convoy, jump in the ditch and pray!" After hours of driving we approach the city of Liège, which is under attack from German V-1s, the flying bombs we call "buzz bombs" because of the loud noise their jet motors make while flying through the air. Much of the city is in ruins.

At last I am under fire. Everyone watches the sky as we move torturously through the debris-filled streets. "There goes one!" is the cry when a buzz bomb is sighted. I find the V-1 awesome to watch, as it is designed so that after a few minutes of flying time the motor suddenly quits and the bomb plunges to the ground. First we hear the sound of the motor, then we spot the flame coming from the rear of the stovepipe-like jet, and then there is a sudden silence, followed shortly by an earthshaking explosion.

"Let's go! Let's get out of here!" The men in the truck often seem beside themselves when the convoy has to halt in the center of the town. The yells grow loudest when one of the V-1s demolishes about half a block of houses less than two blocks from us. Through all of this I feel an interested but very detached observer, a feeling that will stay with me during my first few weeks in combat.

Late in the afternoon we arrive at our destination—a temporary replacement center located in a huge brick factory just outside of Eupen. During the last few hours of the ride we began to hear the distant mutter of artillery over the horizon to the east. With this still in our ears, we stiffly climb down from the trucks and make our way up into the upper stories of the brick factory. Everything in and around the building is inches deep in red brick dust, and none of the hundreds of replacements in the building can take a step without kicking up great clouds of the dust. Even worse, as we try to sleep that night, the movements of the men on the floors above cascades great clouds of brick dust down on us. In order to breathe, we are forced to sleep with our shelter halves over our heads.

Shortly before noon the next day a group of officers, myself included, are told to report to the officer in charge with our equipment. "The following officers over to this side of the road; assigned to the First Division, Price . . ." My reaction: a good outfit from all I have heard. A captain in a trench coat, dirty and unshaven, takes us aside. He does not mince words. "We're catching hell up there. I won't lie to you." He continues, but I do not catch all he says. "Best outfit, oldest outfit, . . . do your part . . . glad to see you . . . need everybody we can get . . . Jerry is determined to come through like he did in the south . . . we are holding the corner."

We load our gear and climb onto First Division trucks. My eyes keep returning to a blond lieutenant who is drinking heavily. During the trip he fires his carbine once—into the air. Soon there is snow on all sides, and we begin to pass through our artillery positions. The guns around us roar unceasingly. Some of the gun emplacements are dug in; other guns evidently have just arrived, but there was no time lost in beginning to fire them. Shells whine overhead as we drive on and on into the snow. Finally, our trucks stop at what appears to be a shattered village crossroad. Frozen, we manage to clamber down from the trucks and enter a shell-torn building.

As we spread our bedding rolls on the floor in an attempt to get warm, we hear a shot in the next room. The blond lieutenant has shot himself in the foot with his carbine. We look at one another silently, thinking, Thank God we did not do that. That was why he was drinking. Working up his nerve. Just as the lieutenant is being carried out to a truck to be evacuated, an excited enlisted man appears in our building. "Come on," he shouts. "Load up on the trucks. They need you at the regiments now!"

We quickly get into the trucks and are off to Camp Elsenborn, which is just behind the division front. The roar of artillery all around us continues, and it is suddenly dark. We are lost. The trucks stop at a church at a crossroad. Crackcrash! We are being shelled with 88s. Crackcrash! They tear your head from your shoulders and they fill the air with screeching fragments. Again I feel detached as I watch the others jump from the trucks into the snow and race to the imagined shelter of the church. I follow into the church, but then a driver shouts, "Can't stay here! Let's get out of here!" There is a mad dash to the trucks, and our driver turns around and races blindly down the roads. Behind us we continue to hear the enemy shells.

We locate a regimental installation in a house. Along with four other lieutenants, I am assigned to 3d Battalion of the 26th Infantry. The officer who gives us this scant information directs us into a kitchen belonging to M Company of my regiment. There the company executive officer tells us to get some food and then bed down anywhere we can find room. Despite the roar of the gasoline stoves, which are busy heating breakfast for the men up front, and the chatter of the cooks and other men present, I am soon sleeping the sleep of exhaustion. I do not realize that it is Christmas Eve.

We are awakened before dawn and taken through the wreckage of the town of Butgenbach. Just on the other side of the town, in the cellar of a wrecked house, is 3d Battalion's command post (CP). We are taken directly to the battalion commander, Lt. Col. John T. Corley, one of the most famous in the army. He impresses me as a hard-eyed man who carefully steels himself to death and mutilation. I later learn that he is a man who fears no one but God, and whose battalion worships the ground over which he leads them.

Colonel Corley repeats each name as the five officers are introduced, then he picks up a sheet of paper and reads off our names. "Price—M Company." I wait to hear something stirring, but he says simply, "You'll join your outfits now. Good luck." Then he leans over his desk and studies his maps. As we salute, my eyes catch a large map behind his desk. A black line comes out sharply to the right and then recedes swiftly to the left bottom of the map. I can tell that we are on the corner, or sharp edge, of the German breakthrough. It also looks suspiciously as though we are out on a limb. But it is not the first time for the First Division, nor, as I will discover, will it be the last.

Lieutenant Quam and I have been assigned to M Company, and we climb into a jeep in front of battalion headquarters and start off to join our unit. We go full speed, as we learn later you always do in combat rides in order to present the fastest moving target possible to the German gunners. We go down a snow-packed road, winding down a valley, and finally stop at the foot of a tree-covered hill. The driver says that this is the Mike Company CP, and we climb out. The jeep quickly drives out of sight, and we are left standing in the road, in the middle of nowhere, and with no one in sight.

Neither of us knows what to do, but finally we hear some talking above us in the forest on the hillside, and so we begin to climb the hill. We are scarcely into the trees when we see signs of activity everywhere. Men are digging holes and carrying things, and there seems to be much hustle and bustle. Everyone who sees us stops and stares. We must look interesting with our closely shaven faces, clean trench coats, and new helmets. We are directed farther up the hill to the company command post and finally find ourselves at the entrance to a long underground bunker. Inside we find two officers sitting at a crude table drinking something from a metal canteen cup. The company commander, Capt. Walter Nechey, is a young giant who looks like a boxer, and was one before the war. He welcomes us to Mike Company, and after asking how things in the United States are going, asks us a few questions about our training in the States. Finally, he tells Lieutenant Quam that he is getting a machine-gun platoon and that I will be assigned to the 81-mm Mortar Platoon. This suits me just fine, inasmuch as I was trained as an artilleryman at the Citadel and have always been fascinated with the larger-caliber weapons. The 81-mm mortar is the front-line artillery of the infantry battalion, employing three second lieutenants as forward observers, who call for and direct the fire of the 81s.

A few minutes later I am a short distance back down the hill at the command post of the mortar platoon, meeting my new boss, Lt. Sam Ciccone. Like all the officers of the division I have met so far, Lieutenant Ciccone is a veteran of North Africa, Sicily, the Normandy invasion, and the fighting in France, Belgium, and Germany. As I meet more and more of these veteran officers and noncommissioned officers of the division, I begin to appreciate the combat skills they possess and the absolute dedication with which they are fighting the long war.

Lieutenant Ciccone, who refers to his platoon as his "lads," is busily engaged in having a larger and deeper platoon headquarters constructed. The position of the mortars just a few yards distant has been heavily shelled in the past few days, and Ciccone has decided that a better CP is in order. I find that he is a strict disciplinarian, but with a heart of gold. As with most of the officers of the division, he is almost afraid to become too friendly with his subordinates for fear that, should they die, their deaths would be that much harder to take. (Later, when I get to know Sam better, he will tell me of the intolerable blow he suffered when a young replacement second lieutenant, much like myself, was killed while carrying out his orders, which took the officer into a spot of particular danger.)

This first meeting with Lieutenant Ciccone is short. He tells me to get rid of my carbine and gives me a .45-caliber pistol in its stead. He briefly explains that as a forward observer, I will have no business fighting the Germans with my weapon but will devote my whole time bringing accurate mortar fire on the Germans. He has me leave my pack and all other excess gear except blankets to the rear, and then tells me that I am to go at once to I Company.

A word should be said here concerning the triangular combat formation used by the infantry. Each infantry division consists of three regiments. Each regiment has three battalions, and each battalion has three rifle companies plus one heavy weapons company. Thus the 3d Battalion of the 26th Infantry consists of rifle companies I, K, and L, and M Company is the heavy weapons company. The heavy weapons company has two machine-gun platoons of "heavies," or water-cooled, .30-caliber machine guns, and one platoon of 81-mm mortars.

At the time I join the 3d Battalion, the battalion is holding the northern corner of the German penetration, with I Company out on Elsenborn Ridge holding the tip, L Company to its left rear several hundred yards, and K Company in reserve on the next hill to the rear of the ridge on which I Company is located. The M Company CP and the 81-mm mortars are on the rear slope of K Company's reserve position.

3

HOLDING THE CORNER

"Normally, you could spend the night here, lad, and I'd send you up tomorrow." Lieutenant Ciccone sounds reluctant to let me go. He tells one of his sergeants to take me up to the front, up to I Company's position. The sergeant, a jeep driver, and I go out of the mortar platoon command post dugout, and get into a jeep parked nearby. I notice that there are sandbags stacked by the side of each wheel. A closer look at the jeep tells me why: there are shell-fragment holes in the hood and through the windshield.

And so my long journey from America as a replacement officer is coming to a close. Soon I will be at the front. It is Christmas Day 1944. We drive along the snow-covered road for about a quarter of a mile and dismount at a blown railway culvert. "We go on foot from here," says the sergeant. "The other section of the mortars is just on the other side of this railroad embankment." We walk through the culvert, and I see four or five mortarmen standing around their mortars. Suddenly they throw themselves to the ground. So does the sergeant. Have they gone crazy? Then I hear it. The rushing, whishing sounds of incoming shells. I spy a depression in the ground and make for it. By this time the shells are already past our position and explode about one hundred yards down the hill behind us. The sergeant eyes me curiously. He knows that I took entirely too long to hit the dirt. I begin to realize the same thing. My first combat lesson is under way.

The men remain on the ground for what seems like minutes. Then another salvo of shells comes over, this time going even farther to the rear and hitting the frozen surface of a large lake. I watch the explosions, which blacken the ice, dig a ragged round hole, and send shivers and cracks coursing through the ice. It reminds me of the effect on an entire puddle top when someone steps onto a thin film of ice on that puddle.

We wait a few minutes longer, and then suddenly everyone is on his feet, going about his business as though nothing happened. Several of the enlisted men at the mortars gather around me. They all try to be friendly, and I can sense their loneliness. They assure me that the "Jerries" have been trying to "find them" all day. They explain that any shell going over their position even the slightest bit high, falls far to the rear due to the sharp drop-off of the slope down to the lake.

Now the sergeant tells me that we had better be off. We have a long way to go, about three miles. We start up the road on the other side of the railroad embankment and begin climbing. The thick pine forest on the hill to our right is silent and foreboding. We see no one. The sergeant sets a fast pace, and soon I am sweating furiously. But on we plod. I am wearing the trench coat I purchased in Givet, a heavy scarf, a sweater, and a field jacket over my woolen uniform. The sergeant notices my predicament and, mercifully, slows down a little.

As we turn left from the road and proceed up a firebreak in the forest, he indicates the position of L Company on our left and tells me of the awful gap between L Company and I Company. I realize what a vast line the battalion is holding. The sergeant takes me to the right end of the L Company line, and I find myself on the forward edge of a ridge, looking across a long valley to another ridge. This new ridge stretches out of sight to the right. From my position I can see that it is the dominating terrain feature of the entire landscape. "Elsenborn Ridge," says the sergeant. He points out a path of footprints stretching straight down the hill in front of me and straight up the far side of the valley. At the bottom a snow-filled creek can barely be seen. A large U.S. Army truck is abandoned in the creek. The sergeant tells me to follow the path to the high ridge and that I will then be in the I Company position. He wishes me luck and starts back in the direction we came from.

I start down the hill, which stretches endlessly away in front of me. At the small stream I stop to examine the truck. It has 99th Division bumper markings; part of the wreckage of a division in retreat. I picture in my mind the truck driver attempting to extricate his truck as it becomes bogged down in the small creek, the furious attempts to free the truck from the mud, and the final quick decision to leave it there and continue on foot.

I pause to adjust my awkward load. In addition to all my other gear, I was given a heavy SCR-300 radio battery to carry with me (I will carry an extra battery in every march or attack we make). Now I start my climb up Elsenborn Ridge. The snow is only about six inches deep. After a long, hard pull, I reach a square field surrounded by a tree line, or hedgerow, as we called it, on all sides. The side of the field running along the ridge top is the front. The tree line extends away to the right, almost the entire length of the long ridge. This is I Company's position.

Entering the rear of the square field I am challenged by a soldier on guard. I give the correct password, and he shows me where the company command post foxhole is located, just about twenty yards up the tree line on the left. In the long, straight hedgerow running along the ridgetop, about seventy-five yards farther on, are the foxholes of the riflemen and machine gunners. At last I am at the front.

I introduce myself to the rifle company commander, Captain Shealy, who tells me that he is glad to see me. I wish him a Merry Christmas and note a look of surprise on his face. He sends for the mortar observer I am to replace. A few minutes later I see a soldier walking from the ridgetop toward me. It is Sgt. George Nestor, a veteran of all of the campaigns of the First Division. I have noticed that almost all of the infantrymen have mustaches, but Nestor's wins the prize. Its ends stand straight out several inches on each side of his face, and he presents a picture of a fierce, athletic fighting man. He greets me warmly and suggests we go right out to his observation post (OP). He also seems startled when I wish him Merry Christmas. He stammers some reply.

It is a beautiful, clear day, extremely cold, but there is visibility for miles in all directions. We pass through the line of foxholes dug in to the hedgerow. To the left and right I see two-man foxholes, manned by the riflemen, usually about ten yards apart. One man normally is making small improvements on the hole, while the other man lies asleep at the bottom of it. I notice that the man on duty frequently stops what he is doing to carefully inspect the field stretching to his front.

Now Sergeant Nestor leads me down a hedgerow that points like a finger down the front slope of the ridge toward the German-held village of Büllingen, in the valley below us. After we have crept cautiously along the hedgerow for about one hundred yards, we come upon a large dugout covered with small logs. This is the observation post, shared by the mortar observer, his radio operator, the field artillery observer, and his radio operator. About ten yards in front is an open foxhole from which we normally observe. Sergeant Nestor takes great pains to instruct me thoroughly in my new duties. He explains how I can call for fire by use of the sound-powered telephone or by using the SCR-300 radio. In the defense the telephone normally is used, as the radio is saved for times when the telephone line has been cut by artillery fire (I find out that this happens often). The OP is on the right side of the hedgerow, and Sergeant Nestor shows me that by crawling through the left side of the hedgerow, I have unrestricted vision of all of the landscape to the north, just as from the OP itself, I have unrestricted visibility to the south.

Since Sergeant Nestor is going to leave me in a few days, he loses no time in teaching me my trade. Through my high-powered binoculars, I search the terrain in front of me. From our position, I can see clearly about half of the town of Büllingen directly in front of us. A series of ridge lines extends to the distant horizon beyond the village. To the right front I see the vital Büllingen-Butgenbach highway leading into our lines. This is the highway the Germans are trying desperately to seize, and the key to its control is the high ridge on which we are located. Through my glasses I can see knocked-out German and U.S. vehicles on the highway.

Shell holes are everywhere I look. The snow is pockmarked. I soon learn the difference between the shell hole left by an artillery shell and that left by a mortar shell. Due to the high angle at which mortar shells are fired, they leave a star-shaped, perfectly geometrical, blackened hole in the snow. The artillery shell, which hits the ground at a much sharper angle, leaves a butterfly-shaped blackened pattern in the snow. Most of the force and destruction of the exploding artillery shell goes out to the sides.

Sergeant Nestor calls for mortar fire on various key points, such as buildings and road junctions, and shows me how to adjust my fire and, most important, how to call for "area fire." This latter term means that your mortars will cover an area about 125 yards square by dropping three rounds at nine equally spaced points within the square. Thus twenty-seven rounds from one mortar or, more commonly, fifty-four rounds from two mortars drop in the target area in less than one minute's time. Nestor tells me that this type of fire is the best answer to an enemy attacking force.

After Sergeant Nestor finishes his lessons, he has me call for and adjust fire. After my lessons are finished, we begin the daily routine of keeping a constant watch for any enemy movement and of trying to keep ourselves warm and contented. Contentment centers around trying to make coffee and finding some method of heating our frozen C-ration cans. The artillery lieutenant has a small mountain stove, and we melt snow for water in a steel helmet. I find that it takes about four helmets full of snow to produce one cup of water, and the process of melting snow is therefore almost continual.

The water in my canteen is frozen solid and remains so for weeks. In addition to the problem of water, there is the problem of trench foot. I find that my feet become numb after about two hours of inactivity and tend to stay that way. The combat boots and woolen socks we wear help very little in keeping our feet warm. We remove our shoes and socks frequently to massage our feet, but even this does not bring full feeling back to our toes.

Late in the afternoon a heavy snow begins to fall, a pattern that will repeat every day for the next two weeks. The snow obliterates all signs of the shelling of the previous day, and the snow grows higher and higher. Now it is dark, and Sergeant Nestor and I leave the observation post and go back along the hedgerow through the front line and proceed to our sleeping hole. We arrive just in time for supper. This is my first experience with the two hot meals we will receive each day. The first is breakfast served from large, insulated cans. Breakfast is served in the dark before daybreak. The noon meal is cold and consists of a can of C rations, which must be eaten in their frosty condition unless we find some way to heat them. The evening meal is hot and, like breakfast, is served in the dark. Unfortunately, almost all of the so-called hot meals I eat are cold by the time I get the food to my mouth. It is an unusual experience to eat two meals a day in the dark standing in the deep snow, often with snow falling on your unseen food. I find that deprived of the sense of sight, and with the food extremely cold, it is difficult to tell what you are eating.

After our supper, George Nestor and I retire to our sleeping hole, which has an overhead cover of small limbs on which about six inches of dirt has been thrown. (In reality, this overhead cover gives us protection from nothing, except possibly the elements, as the smallest caliber shell can easily penetrate it.) George has improvised a small light for the foxhole, using a small flashlight bulb and a piece of tin from a C-ration can for a reflector. His source of power is an old radio battery, and his wiring consists of small pieces of German Army telephone wire. The light from the improvised device is bright enough for us to be able to write letters.

Throughout the night I can hear sporadic German artillery fire falling in various positions on Elsenborn Ridge and on the ridge to our immediate rear. Nevertheless, I am soon sleeping the sleep of the innocent and the uninitiated. The only articles of clothing we remove are our combat boots, which are placed by our side and ready for immediate use. The overcoat over the blanket provides additional warmth. A canvas shelter-half over the entrance keeps our light from showing.

We arise the next morning in the dark and proceed to the mess line, which we can hear but not see, for our breakfast. Fortunately, the coffee served is almost always hot, or at least warm—even if we can't see what we are eating. During the day George continues to instruct me in the technique of being a mortar observer. During the bright morning hours we see considerable air activity, and during all good weather for the next few weeks I often see dogfights between German and Allied fighter planes. With the coming of fairly good weather, we frequently see extremely large formations of bombers proceeding overhead into Germany.

I am surprised on one day to note that the planes passing overhead are dropping what appear to be pieces of tinfoil, which take a long time to reach the ground. I soon find that this is an antiradar device called "chaff," used to defeat German radar installations, and that the pieces of tin are cut to an exact wave length. This tinfoil does much to brighten up the landscape and reminds us of Christmas at home, when foil hangs from the branches of fir and pine trees.

There is considerable V-1 "buzz bomb" activity. It appears that we are on a direct line between a German V-1 launching site and the city of Liège, a major V-1 target. On several occasions, V-1s, also called "flying stovepipes," drop in the division area just to our rear. There is always a sense of fear as a V-1 approaches. When the motor stops, the bomb drops to the ground and explodes. The fear is inspired by not knowing at what moment the motor will stop, causing the bomb to go into its deadly dive.

Now it is my second night at the front. I write my first letter home from the foxhole using the little light that George made. Just before we turn out our light, a terrific shelling of our position begins. German shells are landing all around our foxhole. Many seem to be skimming the top of the hole and dropping into the valley behind us. Suddenly there is an enormous explosion that seems to be in the ground right next to us. In my naïveté I do not feel that the situation is so bad, but I notice that George has a grim expression on his face. He is listening intently as the shells continue to come.

After about half an hour of shelling, the noise ceases. All is quiet except for the crunch of feet in the snow as men move from position to position to give aid to the wounded and to assess the damage done. The next morning I find that two men were killed and one wounded by a direct hit in a foxhole just a few yards from our sleeping hole. On this day George bids me farewell and proceeds back to the mortar platoon headquarters position for a well-deserved rest. I have grown to like George during the two days we have been together, and I feel he richly deserves the battlefield commission he won earlier in December.

Back at my observation post at the first light of day, I began my first day's work on my own. My radio operator is Private Higgins. While observing through my glasses I notice movement on a road that crosses a ridge beyond the German-held town of Büllingen. A closer examination reveals that I am seeing my first German soldier. My glasses make him appear as though he is just a few yards in front of me. He is strolling down a snow-packed road. I decide to bring fire down on him. I call for single rounds of mortar fire at the extreme range and after a few rounds have the satisfaction of seeing him dive into a ditch for cover. He is only the first of many Germans I will see in the next few months.

Now I fall into the daily routine. Up before dawn, taking

my plate through the chow line, shoving a C-ration can in my pocket for lunch, taking a pair of dry socks provided with every breakfast, and moving on up to the observation post. The days blend into one long period of misery alternating with excitement and boredom. I often call for fire on suspicious-looking targets or any enemy movement I see. Occasionally after firing, I have the satisfaction of seeing a German ambulance speed into Büllingen and then depart.

I become extremely friendly with the field artillery forward observers who are with me in the observation post. These young lieutenants are rotated about every three days, and thus there is a continual procession of them into this highly dangerous work. The radio set used by the forward observers is much larger and more powerful than my own set, as theirs has to reach a much longer distance back to the field artillery positions. Normally, I fire at the close-in targets and the artillerymen take over the distant targets.

During this defensive period, two of the forward observers serving with me are seriously wounded. After a few days of my routine I find myself getting rather careless about exposing myself. One day this results in a German mortar round falling directly on top of my observation post. Fortunately, it detonates in the tree branches directly over the log top of the OP and causes no casualties. The noise, however, is tremendous.

The latrine nearest to my sleeping hole is about seventy-five yards up the ridge, almost in the center of the square hedgerow-lined field. This latrine is simply a hole in the ground about four feet long, one foot wide, and four or five feet deep. On one occasion, during daylight hours, as I straddle the latrine with my woolen underpants and trousers pulled down, Jerry sends an 88-mm artillery shell toward our position, which explodes in the air approximately fifty feet directly over the latrine. You can imagine my plight inasmuch as I am unable to move with my pants around my ankles, and to drop to the ground means to drop into the latrine. I remain frozen in my position and am fortunate that none of the shell fragments hit me. I resolve to change my bowel habits, if possible, so that I will not have to use the latrine during the daylight hours.

On another occasion I take my radioman, Higgins, and move to our right about two hundred yards down the long hedgerow on top of the ridge. From here I have better observation of the highways leading north out of Büllingen. Evidently the Germans have seen us make our move, for no sooner have we stopped and dropped into an empty foxhole than an 88-mm shell explodes in the hedgerow almost directly over us. The only casualties are a tree trunk, which is cut in two, and the long, thin, stiff, antenna attached to our radio set. A shell fragment has snipped the antenna neatly into two pieces.

Almost immediately after arriving at the front I begin hearing references to a "Father" Bracken. At first I believe the men are referring to a chaplain, but after a few days, I learn that "Father" Bracken is a corporal assigned to one of the heavy-machine-gun squads of M Company. It is obvious that Father is an almost legendary figure in the 3d Battalion. About a week after arriving at the front I meet Cpl. James J. Bracken. He cuts an almost ridiculous figure. His helmet is pulled down low on his head, which makes his head appear too small, and his face and hands are even dirtier and blacker than those of the other soldiers. His long, brown enlisted man's overcoat is several sizes too large, and it is torn in several places and spotted with mud, dirt, and portions of the innumerable C-rations he has consumed. He wears an outrageously large pair of overshoes over his boots for the extra warmth they give him.

Can this be the fabulous Father Bracken? I ask myself. But

when Bracken opens his mouth and speaks to me for the first time, I immediately sense the reason for his fame. His voice is extremely hoarse, and he speaks with a rush so that his words seem to tumble forth from his lips in an endless gush. His vitality is amazing, and as I get to know him better, I become a staunch friend and admirer of his. He devotes himself to the self-appointed role of lifting the morale of all soldiers with whom he comes in contact—officers and enlisted men alike.

Details of his constant effort to entertain the weary infantrymen in North Africa, Sicily, and during the battalion's fighting on the European continent are told far and wide. I soon see that he spends much of the day and great part of the night moving from foxhole to foxhole, stopping at each to tell a joke, recite original poetry, or sing some original and witty song to the soldiers. Often Father Bracken picks up a telephone and entertains the soldiers in an outpost at the other end of the line. He does this for hours on end, and his repertoire seems to be endless. He wears an infectious grin that is an inspiration and at the same time enormously comic. His nose, like everyone else's nose, seems to run continuously in the bitter cold. But his runny nose forms two white rivulets down his upper lip, which give him an almost clownlike appearance. Yet I can detect the nervousness underlying his magnificent display of humor, and I realize that he has seen too much combat, that he is one of the "older" men on whom the strain of combat seems to take its toll so much more quickly.

As Father Bracken's role of entertaining is very similar to my own desires to share my talents with others, I find myself joining him after dark. We move around the company position and attempt to relieve the boredom and misery of the front line soldier. Father kindly accepts me as a fellow entertainer, and I also find myself broadcasting by telephone, doing imitations and singing songs to some unknown soldiers in their foxholes at the other end of our numerous lines. My favorite imitations at this time are of President Roosevelt, American radio news commentator H. V. Kaltenborn, and a BBC announcer. Of course, I realize that my actions are in great part selfish in that my entertainment of others makes the long hours pass so much more quickly and relieves much of the tension that I am beginning to feel as my days at the front begin to increase.

I am most concerned with the problem of our feet and the lack of mail during this period. The eleventh of November was the last time I received mail. I find myself writing repeatedly on the subject in my letters to my father and mother. In my first letter to my mother from my sleeping hole on the twenty-sixth of December, I write, "How glad I am to finally join these fellows, who so nonchalantly take hell every day, and keep existing. Been directing mortar fire at Jerry for two days. Learning the ropes. Still no mail, but I can wait." On the same day, in a letter to my father, Col. Herbert H. Price, whom I erroneously believe to be still in France with his Third Army medical unit, I write, "Snowy Christmas, and can see for miles around here. Learning my new trade at present, and am becoming proficient. Hope I don't get trench foot."

On the 30th of December I write to my mother,

Wish that mail would catch up with me, as I could sure use some. . . . Snowed hard today, and each snow covers up the shell holes so that on the morning after a snow you'd never know there was a war if it wasn't for the sound. Have been blasting Jerry pretty much, and he blasts back. He certainly has a lot of funny weapons up his sleeve. The dough boys here are certainly the best guys in the world. They are so generous and so awfully friendly. You all freeze alike. The war spares no rank here. Really get a lot of pride here, but my feet sure do get cold. Looks like another year will soon be here. I hope it brings Victory. I am going to do all I can to help it along.

On another quiet day, I scan the distant horizon from my observation post. Behind me I can hear the voices of the artillery forward observer, Lieutenant White, talking to Higgins and the artillery radio operators. Suddenly, on a hill behind Büllingen, I spot some movement. It is in a sparse forest, not more than two miles from us.

I cannot believe my eyes. This is incredible! I am seeing a battery of German field artillery moving into firing position in the open. I rub my eyes and look again. Yes, it is true. One after another, five artillery pieces are trundling into line. I call excitedly back over my shoulder to Lieutenant White. He joins me in a second. I direct him to the target, and we both watch through our glasses. Against the snowy field the men servicing the German guns stand out clearly. The guns seem to point directly at us. "You take it," I say. "It's at extreme range for me." Lieutenant White answers hastily, "You bet I will! This is the artillery man's dream target." In a matter of seconds he has a fire mission sent back through his own radio set to the 33d Field Artillery, which is in continual support of the 26th Infantry Regiment.

In a few seconds his radio operator calls forward to us that the first round is on the way. Realizing that the German artillery pieces can begin firing at any second, our tension grows. Perhaps we are the target! Our first 105-mm round seems to fall far to the rear of the German artillery pieces. Lieutenant White calls back an immediate correction, and the radio operator calls forward that there will be a delay. On hearing that it is a German field artillery battery, the 33d is calling for the heavy 155-mm artillery pieces of another field artillery battalion to add their fires to the target. Lieutenant White carefully checks his computations and again gives the correction that will put both battalions on the target. We wait minutes that seem hours, and then at last the message comes: "On the way!"

Behind us we can hear our artillery pieces fire almost in unison. Almost immediately we hear high above our heads the swishing sound of outgoing artillery shells headed for the target. Through our glasses we watch the shells hit. The firing is perfect. Shells strike between, in front of, and behind the German artillery pieces. We can see the German artillerymen hitting the ground, jumping up, and running around. It must be quite an experience to be hit with fire minutes after having occupied a new firing position.

Lieutenant White calls for the fire again and again. Now we see incredible bravery and discipline on the part of the Germans. With shells raining down on them, they hitch up their artillery pieces once more to their vehicles and quickly disappear back in the direction from which they originally came. We can see the bodies of several German artillerymen left in the snow and congratulate each other that one German artillery piece remains behind—obviously out of commission. White follows the now-invisible column with shrewdly directed fire for several minutes after it disappears.

I am at my observation post when a new company commander comes forward to the front line of foxholes of his company. I watch him curiously while he searches the terrain to his front, spots the distant rooftops of Büllingen, throws his carbine to his shoulder, and fires several shots in the direction of the enemy. A look of satisfaction seems to come across his face as he demonstrates his defiance of the Germans, and he turns and walks back to his command post. In all the nearby foxholes we pull our heads down as far as we can. We do not like anyone disturbing the status quo.

On another day, I see a small group of soldiers moving up to the forward line of foxholes of I Company behind me. As it is quiet, I decide to move back to see what is going on. I find that it is the commanding general of my division, Major General Huebner, and my regimental commander, Colonel Seitz, visiting the front. The division commander's aide-de-camp carries a submachine gun and looks ready for business.

And so, each day the snow becomes deeper and the temperature drops. One day, near the end of my stay with I Company, we see a messenger making his way to our observation post carrying a small bundle of white cloth under his arm. "Here's your snow suits," he says. We examine the white cotton cloths he has given us with great interest. There is one small piece of bed sheet about two feet square that is placed over the helmet and tucked in underneath. The other piece of bed linen is considerably larger and has a hole cut in the center through which we are to slide our helmet and head. There are white tapes sewn along the sides that are used to fasten the sheet around us.

Some of the riflemen tear pieces of the sheets into strips and camouflage their rifles by winding the sheet around the M-1s. This is the American Army's answer to the fighting in the snow. We discuss this newest "secret weapon" with some sarcasm. Evidently, rumors that the United States expected the war to be over before Christmas were true. We wonder what Belgian towns were asked to surrender their bed sheets in order that we could have camouflage. Nevertheless, we don the strange apparel and wear it until the snow melts.

During this period we learn that the mess personnel are having more and more difficulty breaking their way through the snow to bring our rations and ammunition forward to the front from the kitchen miles to the rear. Also, we find that it is extremely difficult for litter bearers to evacuate casualties. Yet there appears another "secret weapon"—one that actually does the job. It is a vehicle about the size of a jeep, which, instead of wheels, has full tracks similar to a tank. Called the "weasel," this is the only vehicle that will traverse the deep snow. Unfortunately, our battalion has only one weasel, and it is kept extremely busy bringing forward supplies and evacuating our casualties. We all are extremely happy that we have the weasel and praise the unknown inventor of this very practical machine.

As the temperature continues to drop each day and high winds begin to make the temperature seem even colder, we are forced into "bundling," an expedient for warmth at night. Each night my radio operator and I huddle as close to each other as possible and draw what blankets we have around our bodies to keep out the cold. Higgins tells me on several occasions that I am as warm as a hot-water bottle. I cannot say the same for Higgins, who seems to be a cold-blooded person. He lends me very little body warmth while we are sleeping. Nevertheless, I am grateful for what little added warmth this brings, and we continue to sleep together in our sleeping holes until the bad weather abates.

On another day, a mortar round hits near our observation post and Lieutenant White takes a tiny shell fragment through the neck. He remains on his feet, through he turns extremely pale. His radio operator walks with him to the rear. On another night, another forward observer serving with me is wounded while splicing telephone wire in the rear of our position. This is an unending task at which we all take our turns.

On the twenty-eighth of December the Germans launch a major attack on the left of our position up the railroad embankment in the valley. The attack is repulsed by L Company on our left and some of the I Company riflemen on the left side of our position. There are many German dead from this attack, and it takes several days before the snow completely covers their bodies. One arm sticking up through the snow is visible for several days to the left front of my observation post.

During this defensive period we have many cases of "trench foot." One day I am visited by Lt. Jack "Sunshine" Lewis, a Citadel classmate of mine who commands the platoon of 60-mm mortars of I Company. He complains as usual that he cannot feel his toes and pulls off one combat boot. Then, when he pulls off his sock, several of his toes come with the cloth, leaving several naked toe bones exposed. Without saying a word of complaint, Lieutenant Lewis pulls the sock back onto his foot, puts his foot into his combat boot, bids me farewell, and starts limping to the rear to receive medical attention. He is an extremely brave officer. I never see him again during the war.

In a New Year's letter to my mother, I write, "I wish I could think up a way to keep the Infantry's feet warm for the next war. The reason I can write today is that I was sent to the rear for a rest and am warm and indoors. Of course I have to go back up this evening, but this was a blessed break. Gives my feet a chance to thaw and my eyes a chance to rest. I use field glasses all day, it seems."

On the fourth of January I get a chance to change my long underwear. In a letter to my mother, I write, "Was told to come back from my front of the front office to the rear and on arriving at 'M' Company CP (Command Post) I was given the opportunity to shave, wash, and even get my longies changed. I was still wearing a pair that I had put on back in the States. For the past few days I thought Jerry was using a new gas. Then I discovered that it was me! It snows every day and gets deeper." The next day I write to my father, "A very quiet day here. Of course at other points along the long line guys may be sweating out a push, but here there is comparative peace. The sun is out and glistening on the deep snow. The artillery still pounds away and the planes drone overhead but Jerry is quiet across the way. I haven't gotten that mail yet, but I am really sweating it out and expect some any day."

I find on these two trips that the mortar platoon headquarters was shelled so severely that they had to improve drastically the protection of their command post. They chopped down a number of pine trees and created an underground bunker that was almost impervious to all but a direct hit of a major-caliber artillery shell.

On the twelfth of January I am rotated back to the reserve company position for a rest. Here I find a vacant dugout and fortunately am issued a liquor ration consisting chiefly of a bottle of Cognac and two bottles of French champagne. I share this booty with my radioman, the field artillery observer, and their radiomen. I occupy myself in this position by attempting to light a small Belgian stove that was placed by some previous occupant in the bottom of the dugout. While trying to light the coal in the stove, I decide to use some gasoline. The resulting fire in the dugout drives me rather rapidly from it and singes my field jacket. But I am taught a valuable lesson about trying to light fires with gasoline.

I write my mother, "Yesterday was the second month with no mail. We are certainly having the snows, and the stuff is waist deep in spots. Very cold, bitter weather for fighting, but fight we must." The following day I again write my mother: "So again I scrawl my message of love to you and reassure you that your little boy is O.K. and that he is keeping his feet dry. The wind has been blowing great hunks of snow from the pines today and the tops of some of the heavily laden trees have come crashing down. Some are brought down by artillery, and so you see that we keep dodging." On the same day I write my father, "Things are quiet here, and the snow piles up, and the men get trench foot regularly. . . . I still have had no mail. Sort of thought that it could come quicker from you. Don't let the cold get you down. I am happy, healthy, and stink like hell. Wish the govt. would invent a padded, warm shoe."

After this short rest in the reserve company position I am assigned to L Company, which is holding the left side of the battalion position. I also get a new radio operator, Private First Class Potts, from Aliceville, Alabama. Now I meet the company commander of L Company. He is Captain Ritter, a calm soldier and easily the most competent and admired company leader in the battalion. His pet word is *merci,* which he pronounces "mercy." I find that everyone in the battalion uses the word *beaucoup.*

The aerial activity increases as the weather becomes better. One day I see about nine hundred B-17 bombers in the air in one massive flight. Also during this period I am hit for the first time by enemy fire. Fortunately, the shell fragment passes through the deep snow before it strikes my leg. It is so slowed down that it does not cut through my combat boot.

And on the fifteenth of January the mail finally comes! From my forward observation post on the hill overlooking Büllingen, I write this letter:

15 JANUARY 1945
BELGIUM

My dearest Mother and Father, and how happy I am to be able to write those five words again.

This is one of the happiest days of my life. Today I received six letters from you, and the last one that you wrote was the one that brought the good news.

Boy, that was the one worry that I had in this world. That of getting either Dad or Hick [my brother, an artillery lieu-

tenant who has been in the South Pacific since January 1942]
home to be with mother. And so the old war horse [my father]
is home at last. Boy, that is *swell*. Of course the letter was
written on Dec. 20, and left a lot of questions but I am sure
that I will have them answered in the next few letters. . . . Boy
oh boy, I'm so damn happy for Dad's sake, and your sake, and
Sugar's sake [Sugarfoot is our Italian greyhound dog, the sole
companion of my mother during the war], and for Hick's peace
of mind and mine. As long as I know that the Guvnor is there
to look after you, Mommy, you who have caught so much more
hell that the rest of us. So Dad sang in the shower. How does
it feel to take a shower, Dad? . . . Today Jerry tried to bracket
me with his mortars but I didn't give a damn. I was happy, so
I threw about 75 rounds back at him and came back down the
hill to borrow this paper to write my happiness!!

Bye, bye,
Pres

On the twenty-second of January I receive a twenty-four-hour
pass to go back to the Belgian town of Verviers. It is snowing
when I get into a truck already loaded with soldiers who are
also going on the pass. The day is bitterly cold, and the men
stamp their feet for warmth. A medic is passing out sulfa tablets;
he says they will prevent venereal disease. I decline.

After an hour's ride we arrive. I go to a Belgian restaurant
in Verviers and order the best meal they have. It consists of a
horse-meat steak with French fried potatoes, and I stuff myself
on the delicious food. Next I ask directions to a barber shop as
my hair has grown exceedingly long. I am mildly surprised to
find that the barber is a Belgian lady who does not seem to know
her trade very well. In altogether too short a time, the pass is
finished and I am mounting the truck again to proceed back to
the front.

We sit in the truck on the ride back, all of us with a sinking feeling in the pits of our stomachs. We all noted the tremendous increase in the distant artillery fire during the brief time we were in Verviers. As we drive back through the field artillery positions in the rear of our lines, we realize that the artillery activity has intensified. On our arrival in the battalion area, we find that the 2d Infantry Division has taken over our portion of the line and that our regiment has moved into an assembly area near Camp Elsenborn to prepare to launch an attack to drive the Germans out of the Bulge.

4 ☆

THE ATTACK

Immediately after arriving at my unit's assembly area, I am summoned to the company commander's post, a hole like any other, to receive the attack order. We attack at dawn, tomorrow, the twenty-fourth of January.

A sleepless night in a hole, and then off to join L Company for the attack. I like this because the company commander, Captain Ritter, is the best. First the long march from Elsenborn to Butgenbach, then the long delays caused by action at the Dom Butgenbach. In Butgenbach the men are freezing, and suddenly they decide to do something about it. A group in front of me gathers in the ruins of a house and builds a fire in the bathtub. The smoke is terrible, but some are so cold that they brave the smoke and huddle over the tub. I see Sherman tanks skating down the ice-covered highway, tons of steel with brakes locked, sliding with ever-increasing momentum down the hill, one after another, looking like brown toys in the distance. Some end up in the ditch, others miraculously survive, pointed in the right direction at the hill bottom.

The order comes to move out again. The column stretches a mile in front of me and a mile behind me. Now we are passing Dom Butgenbach, just one or two buildings in rubble, with Jerry's barbed wire just beyond. One of our tanks hits a mine and one of its tracks is blown off. The rumor passes that it hit our own mines buried before the snow fell, and just now thawed to the extent that the pressure of the tank treads could explode them.

We turn off the road to the right and start across a wide field about three feet deep in snow. We follow in the tracks of the men ahead of us. Blazing the trail must have been hell on the leading scouts. My load is almost intolerable. I am carrying my extra radio battery under one arm in addition to all of the other equipment and my trench coat. Finally we leave the field and start up a high series of hills, all densely forested. An occasional mortar round hits far ahead of us. Up and up we go through the deeply drifted snow, stumbling, unable to see the logs, sticks, and rocks under the snow. It is sometimes necessary to crawl over fallen trees. The company I am with now turns slightly left toward the north and begins to attack toward a crossroad, somewhere to our front. For some reason, the crossroad is known as Paratroop Cross Roads. I later discover that we are attacking the 1st Battalion of the 1055th Volksgrenadier Regiment, a distinctly nonparatroop outfit.

Now I have fallen slightly behind the men in front of me and seem to be out of touch with the men behind me. I am alone following a trail in the snow. Where is everybody? Suddenly I hear a sound to my left. A German soldier is crawling toward me. He is saying something, over and over. He is wounded, and he is saying, "Wasser! Wasser! Wasser!" A sort of panic overtakes me at this sight of my first German at close range. "No, no, no!" I say in German. "Go back, go back, that way!" I point back down the trail. The German reaches out with his hand, pleading with me and making motions as if he is drinking from a canteen. I brush past him, swearing, and shout at him to go back down the trail. I pass on without looking behind me. I know that the first-aid men are at the rear of the column. They will take care of him. Thus, I clear my conscience. Now I catch up with the file in front of me.

Suddenly we are in a clearing with a main road cutting through the woods in front of us. The men in front of me have flushed up a German. He runs across the road. The men shout, "There he is! Get him! Get him!" The German is joined by about ten other Germans running across the road to the forest on the other side. Now the firing is general, as every rifleman is taking potshots at the Germans. Some are firing as fast as their rifles can fire. The sound of the empty clips pinging into the air as the last round of eight is fired makes a musical sound strangely at variance with the harsh echoing sound of the rifles firing.

Some of the Germans are hit and fall. Others run a little farther then kneel with their hands in the air. The firing continues for a few seconds, then the Germans are quickly rounded up. We find that we are at a small crossroads and just a few yards from it is a German command post bunker. In almost no time, our soldiers, who have fanned out and crossed the road, begin to appear back on the road with prisoners, and about fifteen are collected. I walk over to them. One is sitting on a stump, keening to himself and rocking back and forth. He is shot through both thighs, and the blood is beginning to seep through his white camouflage uniform pants.

Now a German aid man points to the wounded man with his fingers, which are clasped across the top of his helmet, just as are the hands of all of the prisoners. The aid man points to

3rd Bn 26th Inf Attacks During the Battle of the Bulge

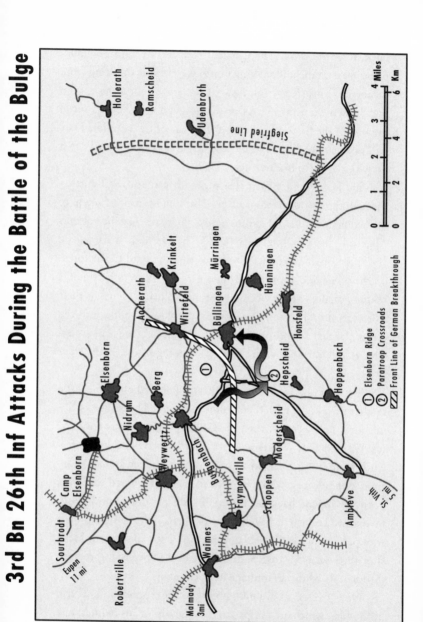

Hollerath
Ramscheid
Udenbroth
Siegfried Line

Krinkelt
Aocherath
Wirtzfeld
Büllingen
Mürringen
Hünningen
Honsfeld
Heppenbach

Elsenborn
Berg
Nidrum
Weywertz
Büdgenbach
Faymonville
Moderscheid
Schoppen
Amblève

Camp Elsenborn
Sourbrodt
Eupen 11 mi
Robertville
Waimes
Malmady 3mi

St. Vith 5 mi

Hepscheid

① Elsenborn Ridge
② Paratroop Crossroads
▨ Front Line of German Breakthrough

4 Miles
Km

0   1   2   3
0   2   4   6

his medical kit, and then to the man, several times, until finally he walks over to the wounded man, helps him pull his trousers down, and inspects the wounds. He begins to put first-aid dressings on the legs, and some of the other Germans watch. It is a tableau of men, German and American, standing in the snow, looking at each other, with no motion, and no words. Only the aid man is doing something. Now another German prisoner begins to point at his backside, with downward shoveling motions. Everyone knows what this means. He has to defecate. I nod my head. The German man immediately drops his pants and squats. Yes, it is diarrhea. Now others make motions requesting to do the same or to urinate. This they do.

I notice one prisoner is as white as a ghost and leans more and more against a comrade. He slumps to the snow, and we see the blood running down his hand from under his jacket sleeve. One of our sergeants places two men in charge of the prisoners, and I turn to go on into the forest on the other side of the road. We hear firing again to our front. I come to an edge of the forest and gaze across a small valley that is cleared of all trees.

A horse-drawn military vehicle is attempting to flee across the opposite hillside on a small road. Our soldiers have opened up on the wagon with rifles and automatic rifles. Suddenly someone shouts, "Cease fire! Don't shoot! Ambulance! Don't shoot." But the vehicle is riddled. The horses scream, a sound that carries easily through the clear of the beautiful snow scene, even though the wagon is about two hundred yards from us. Our soldiers swear horribly—no one wanted to hurt the horses, although men are a different story. A sergeant takes his squad on the run toward the wagon. He shouts something about "putting them out of their misery." A few minutes later several shots ring out. The horses have stopped screaming.

Now the business of consolidation of the position we have seized begins automatically. We take up positions at the edge of the cleared field, and most of us find German foxholes, which are immediately taken for our own use. It is impossible to dig in the frozen ground, and later we hear blocks of TNT being detonated by some of our men who try to break up the frozen topsoil. My hole contains the usual quota of litter—old letters, ration cans, and the like—left by the previous occupants.

I walk back up the hill to the crossroads to see what assistance I can be to the company commander. At the crossroads I find that the large bunker was also used as a first-aid station, and that nearby in the woods there is a stack of at least twelve dead German soldiers. I see some of our soldiers breaking the German rifles against pine trees in order to render them useless in case a German counterattack retakes this position. This looks like fun, so I too step over and pick up a German rifle and proceed to bend it as much as possible around a sturdy pine. I find that it is easy to break the wooden stock but another matter to try to bend the barrel. As I am engaged in this task I look up to find my platoon leader, Lieutenant Ciccone, watching me with a camera in his hands. He asks me to pose for him, and I oblige, holding one of the German rifles in my hands.

A heavy snow begins to fall, and when I leave the bunker a few minutes later, after finding out the general direction from which the company commander feels the Germans will counterattack, I find that the body of a German soldier who was killed in our attack is now half-covered with snow. I know I shall not easily forget the sight of the skyward staring eyes and gaping mouth, now filled with snow, and the body rapidly disappearing from sight under the huge snowflakes.

I have only been gone from the new company command post for a few minutes when I hear the sickening crump of mortar shells falling very close to it. I pay no attention to the shelling, which ceases as quickly as it began, and proceed to my new observation post. A few minutes later a messenger from the L Company commander arrives and tells me that one of the mortar rounds hit and killed Capt. Seth Botts, the battalion operations officer. Captain Ritter wants to know if I can do something about the German mortars. I tell the messenger that I was unable to hear the German mortars fire, but that I will certainly bring them under fire if I can locate them. As usual, I can not hear the enemy weapons fire.

I get my radio going and find out that my mortars are set up several hundred yards behind me on the other side of the crossroad. I go through the registration of fires procedure that I will employ after every attack or advance from now until the end of the war. I have one of the mortars fire at various points to our front, which appear to be the most likely avenues of approach of a German attack. I "walk" these mortar rounds in toward me, until a round lands only seventy-five yards in front of our line. Over the radio I tell my mortar crew, "Mark that one as Concentration One." I mark about six such concentration points, placing their numbers and locations on my map. Now I am in business.

Shortly after dark I am in my foxhole—which, incidentally, is coated top, bottom, and sides with about three inches of ice from the breath condensation of the previous occupant—when a runner comes from the company commander requesting my presence immediately. I am up and out in the snow in a matter of seconds, since the only clothing I have removed is my boots. I walk back up through the trees to the bunker and notice that the dead German on the path is now completely covered, although the snow ceased in the late afternoon.

The company commander tells me that his listening posts

have heard sounds in a small clump of tall trees located in the open field. I immediately recognize the feature, as I zeroed one mortar concentration on that point during the afternoon just in case. A few minutes later my radio operator and I are back at the edge of the clearing, and I order the mortars to fire a twenty-seven-round concentration, which covers an area one hundred yards square, directly into the clump of trees. Because of the previous registration, it is not necessary for me to fire a registration round at all, and the Germans, if there are any there, suddenly, and without warning, have twenty-seven rounds of mortar fire dropping on their heads. I soon receive a report that all sound from that target has ceased. A patrol the next day reports finding a few foxholes started in the clump, but nothing else of interest.

The next morning, after finishing my breakfast, which is a C-ration can of baked beans heated rather inadequately over a small German field stove, I walk back up to the company command post. Here I notice for the first time that the main highway we captured the day before is literally covered with large pine trees that the Germans felled using explosives tied around the tree trunks. The highway is covered with fallen trees for approximately 150 yards to the right of our position.

As I arrive at the command post, a large engineer bulldozer comes thrashing up the trail over which we attacked and appears at the command post. The driver is a giant of a man, and he calls out as soon as he arrives, "Are these the trees you want moved?" Captain Ritter tells him that all the trees must be moved so our tanks can get through. "Watch out for mines!" Ritter adds. "We haven't cleared the road under these trees."

The bulldozer operator, who is chewing gum, replies, "I don't give a damn about mines." He turns his bulldozer toward the giant trees and begins to throw the blade of his vehicle against first one and then another. When I leave to go back to my observation post a few minutes later, I see that the bulldozer operator has made good progress in pushing the fallen trees to the side of the road and has already cleared about one-fourth of the trees from the highway. I leave with his curses, directed toward his giant machine, ringing in my ears.

During our wait at Paratroop Cross Roads we are issued the new "snow-pacs." These are felt-lined boots with an additional half-inch felt insert to go under the foot. We are told that they are guaranteed to keep our feet warm. We hasten to put them on and turn in our leather combat boots, which are carefully collected and hauled to the rear for use in the spring. I find that the snow-pacs keep my feet much warmer than the combat boot when we are in a stationary position.

On the twenty-eighth of January we receive our orders: the battalion will attack the town of Büllingen. I am pleasantly surprised to get this order as I am fully aware that the main German defenses of Büllingen were on the northern side of the town facing Elsenborn Ridge, which we defended for so long. This attack will come from the south, and we will be able to enter Büllingen by the back door, so to speak. We all devoutly hope that the defenses on the south side will be much weaker. Another bit of good news: L Company will not lead this attack.

We begin the approach march just after dark. The battalion assembles on the highway, and there are long delays before L Company finally begins its march. The snow reflects enough light so that we can see for approximately two hundred yards. It appears that the attack will be made with no artillery preparation. Just in front of L Company I can hear some of our tanks moving in the column.

We march down the highway for about half a mile and then leave the highway, turning right into alternating forest and fields.

Now the most grueling part of the attack begins. First march. Then we stand and wait. We find that the new snow-pacs make our feet sweat excessively and that the sweat saturates the felt inserts. Then when we stand, often for half an hour without moving, in snow that ranges from knee to waist deep, the sweat freezes and our feet become unbearably cold. Now we move again; then once more we wait.

Once we leave the highway it is necessary for each man to follow in the tracks of the man in the front of him. Much of the delay is caused by the fact that the leading men in each single-file column must be alternated frequently as they become exhausted in just a few minutes. The mutter of artillery in all directions continues without abatement, as it has ever since I came to the front.

We have marched perhaps a mile and a half; it has taken us hours. Now we hear firing at the head of the column. The leading company is catching it. Soon we can hear rifle and machine-gun fire. Then we hear heavier explosions of mortar and artillery shells. Every few minutes I turn to Potts, who follows me five yards behind, and ask him to test the radio. Something is wrong. Probably the mouthpiece is frozen or else some other part of the radio has become frozen in the intense cold. We are unable to raise anyone by radio. We move on.

Marching directly in front of me is a heavy-machine-gun squad from M Company, which is attached to L Company for this attack. Now we move into a forest. Suddenly a German "burp gun" fires a staccato burst to our left. The German sub-machine gun has such a rapid rate of fire that the bursts sound almost like someone tearing canvas. Bullets snap through the trees above our heads. We dive into the snow the moment we hear the firing, and fortunately, no one is hit. The riflemen and machine gunners in the snow stare up to the left through the trees. "Where is he?" "Do you see him?" "Where is that bastard?" The burp gun is silent, and slowly the long single-file column arises and moves steadily forward again.

I notice an officer breaking his way through the snow about five yards to my left. He seems in a hurry to get to the head of the column. As he comes closer I recognize him as Lieutenant Colonel Murdoch, the new 3d Battalion commander. I wonder to myself what he is like. He will have a hard time replacing Colonel Corley, who has finally been rotated to the States. Now, nearer, the German burp gun again opens fire on us. As I dive for the snow, it is with satisfaction that I see the battalion commander doing the same. There is some pleasure in finding that even high-ranking officers have the same reactions as the rest of us. I notice, however, that Colonel Murdoch is up and moving forward long before the rest of us.

Shortly after we begin moving again, German mortar shells begin to hit our column. Now the small-arms fire ahead reaches a crescendo. We continue to move forward in single file. Now we are out of the forest and in open fields. We move through gaps in barbed wire fences that surround the small fields. The lead men have cut a path through the barbed wire. I step on an unseen object beneath my feet in the snow. My foot turns under me and I find myself thrown heavily into the snow. I have sprained my ankle badly. There is nothing to do but get up, which I quickly do. I find that after a few yards the pain begins to subside. Potts is asking me if I am all right. I reassure him.

Now the mortar shells exploding around us begin to afford us better illumination. Those striking in the hedgerows, which border the fields, are tree bursts and spray their hot fragments of metal in all directions. Behind me and in front of me from time to time I can see men being hit. They crawl a few yards out of the path into the snow. The cry "Medic!" is passed up and down the line, but the line continues to move forward. In the illumination of the bursting mortar shells, I see that there is another single-file column marching parallel to us on the other side of the field. Again I trip over something in the snow and am thrown heavily to my knees. Again I struggle to my feet. The snow is soft and yielding. This time Potts seizes my arm and assists me. There is no chance to stop or to take cover from the shelling; we must move on.

The attack takes on all aspects of a nightmare. I lose all track of time. In the middle of the field to my right I see something, or someone, crawling. In my imagination it is a German. The object that I see points a rifle in my direction. I call to the soldiers in front of me. "See that German out there! There! There! Don't you see him! Shoot him! Shoot him!" The soldiers look in the direction I point but appear to see nothing and continue to trudge straight ahead through the snow. Again I look to the right, but this time I see nothing moving in the snow.

A few minutes later I see what appears to be an antitank gun in the snow to the right. As I come closer to it, I realize that it is the tongue of a wagon protruding from the snow. My imagination is playing all sorts of tricks on me. Now the mortar fire on the column increases. A few soldiers ahead of me I see a soldier drop to the snow by the side of the path. He is sitting up. When I draw abreast of him, I see that it is Father Bracken.

"What's the matter, Father?" Are you hit?"

"I can't make it, Lieutenant. I want to go on, but I can't make it." I can see in the illumination of bursting shells that his face is pale under the usual grime that covers it. I plead with him to get to his feet and get back in the column. But I can stay here no longer. I can see by the blank look in Bracken's eyes that threats or cajolery will not move him.

"You'll be all right, Corporal. Just rest here a few minutes. You'll be okay."

Potts and I struggle through the deep snow, at the side of the path, trying to catch up with our place in the column. Once again my weakened ankle gives way beneath me and I am thrown head-first into the deep snow. Once again Potts assists me to my feet. And still the radio will not work. Now a faint light appears over the distant horizon. Dawn is beginning to break, and in a few minutes it will be light. If the Germans catch us in the fields they will be able to mow us down. The column quickens its pace, and soon we can make out the first building on the edge of the town.

Now our column moves through a gap in a hedgerow at the end of a field. Just in front of us we see the first building of the town. The field beyond the trees is under intense mortar fire. I hear Potts, directly behind me, calling to me. He shouts, "We can't go in there!" I immediately reply, "Oh, yes we can, Potts. Come on! We're too exposed here. It'll be better in the buildings."

We move on. It gets lighter each minute. I find a large number of riflemen huddled around the walls of the house. Captain Ritter is standing outside it, giving rapid orders to his attacking squads. The men around the house are from the leading company, which has suffered heavy casualties from German machine-gun and mortar fire. From inside the house I hear pitiful shrieks and moans. Someone tells me that the leading company caught hell.

Captain Ritter seems to realize that we must push on before daylight or we will suffer more casualties. And so L Company continues the attack into the town. As the attacking squads disappear on each side of the main street running through the town, the sound of small-arms and machine-gun fire increases.

Potts follows me as I move toward the left-hand row of houses. In front of me, moving toward me, is a stretcher with a wounded man on it carried by four stretcher bearers. In the half-dark I can see that they are slipping in the snow. Suddenly there comes the slithering swish of an incoming shell. It strikes the snow about ten yards to my left and about fifteen yards from the stretcher. Everyone hits the ground and I instantly feel a tremendous blow as a fragment of the shell slaps into my boot. It is as though someone has hit me on the leg with a hammer. Once again the deep snow has slowed the fragment down and I am not wounded. As I get to my feet I see the stretcher bearers working the wounded soldier back on to the litter. Now I break into a limping run for the first house on the left. More shells continue to come in. As I move from house to house, rushing rapidly from one sheltering wall to another down the long street, I realize that it is daylight.

In crossing a vacant lot between two houses I am brought up short by an unusual sight. There appear to be five piles of snow equally spaced in a straight line across the lot. I move closer to the first pile and discover that it is one of our riflemen wearing his snow camouflage sheet. He is crouched on both knees—dead. Bright red blood has congealed on the side of his face. It is the same with the next four riflemen. They have been hit by machine-gun fire and stopped in their tracks. All of them are kneeling or crouching. None are out flat on the snow.

I realize I have outdistanced Potts, who is carrying the heavy radio. I rush into a large barn and run to the center of the room. There in front of me, at the corner of two walls, stands a German soldier. Both his feet and arms are spread apart slightly as though he is trying to push himself back into the corner of the barn. He stares straight at me. I grab for my pistol but do not draw it as the German makes no move whatsoever. Then in the dim light I make out the saffron-colored skin that indicates death. Now I see the hole in his forehead just between his eyebrows from which a small trickle of blood drips down one side of his face. He is frozen in his standing position.

This German shocks me. I begin to think I am dreaming. I rush back out of the barn in time to see that Potts has come up. We make our way from house to house, moving always toward the sound of the firing ahead of us. Now the sounds of machine-gun fire on the outskirts of the town cease. Evidently we have broken the line of German resistance.

I pass the door of a large stone house. Some L Company riflemen are standing there. Over the sound of the shell fire and small-arms fire I can see that they are listening to the shrill ringing of a German telephone. "There's a Jerry phone in there ringing, Lieutenant," they say. "Why don't you answer it?" I think rapidly. If an American answers the phone this may bring German artillery fire on the town in immediate answer. I tell the riflemen, "Better leave it alone. Let it keep ringing." Potts and I move on.

In the center of the town I find Captain Ritter. He has taken over the cellar of one of the large houses as his command post. In all directions we see our soldiers herding in small groups of German prisoners. Once L Company penetrated the town, resistance collapsed. Because of the occasional incoming artillery shells, prisoners and captors alike huddle close to the sides of the houses.

Up the main street I see several white phosphorus rounds land. They fill the street, first with their vivid streak of orange fire, then with billowy stinking clouds of white smoke. Some of the soldiers in front of us scream out as the white-hot phosphorus burns their skin. Captain Ritter rushes forward to see that the burned men are given aid. I rush after Captain Ritter, telling him that I will move on to the front of the town to see if I can find any retreating Germans to shell as they pull out of town. He nods agreement.

Potts and I move steadily forward, and when we reach the far end of the town we find that the small-arms fire has ceased. German artillery shells continue to burst in and around the town. I discover that the front end of the town ends just before the railroad embankment. From the end house, which stands in ruins, as does almost every other house in the town, I find a window that overlooks the entire northern landscape. Again I have Potts try the radio, and this time we are able to make contact with the mortar platoon.

Now I begin my observation of the hills rising in front of me in the direction that the Germans are retreating. At first I see nothing moving, but I continue to scan the terrain with my glasses. I have a funny feeling about this observation post because the house stands so high and isolated. Worse, it has no cellar. Sure enough, as soon as I think this, several artillery rounds land around the house in quick succession. Potts and I throw ourselves to the floor against the front wall of the house. Looking up, I find myself staring through an enormous hole in the ceiling through which the beautiful blue sky is visible. One round hits the back side of the house with an enormous explosion. We are covered with dust but otherwise unhurt. As soon as the shelling stops, I am back at the window again scanning the terrain.

At a distance of about a mile, to my left front, I begin to see signs of movement. Some Germans are digging in a hedgerow on a hillside. They have evidently only just begun to dig, as

I can see that their bodies are still above the surface of the ground. I take them under fire with the mortars and have the satisfaction of seeing some of my rounds fall in or extremely close to the hedgerows. I report this target by radio to the mortar platoon and continue to shell the hedgerow for about an hour until there is no more sign of digging there.

A runner comes to my position and tells me that Captain Ritter wants me to come to the command post to question some prisoners. I move back through the village smelling the unmistakable stench of town fighting. There is the smell of burning wood, the disagreeable, pungent odor that white phosphorus gives off, the smell of high explosive, and feces and manure. After questioning several German noncommissioned officers and privates I realize that they probably know nothing of the general situation. All are in agreement that things look very bad for Germany. Our attack through the back door of the town took them by surprise. Captain Ritter releases me. He looks dead tired.

On leaving the command post I see the long column of German prisoners gathering to march out of the town to the rear. I count two hundred of them in the column. A real bag! I walk over to one prisoner who is wearing the usual German snowsuit. It consists of a beautifully quilted, warm jacket and pair of quilted trousers. The pieces are reversible, a mottled camouflage design on one side, white on the other. I direct Jerry to take off his snow trousers, as I very much want them for the warmth and camouflage they will give. He obliges me, and I see that he has on his regulation greenish grey woolen trousers under the snow trousers. I get into the snow trousers and walk around the building looking at the numerous pieces of German field equipment lying on the ground. I am attracted to a German helmet and so take off my helmet and put the German helmet on my head. Without thinking, I now stroll around the corner of the building into the main street.

Instantly several riflemen point their rifles at me and yell "Halt!" I freeze in my tracks and begin to call loudly that it is me, Lieutenant Price, not a Jerry. The men recognize me and begin to laugh. I throw the German helmet from my head, determined never to make such a mistake again. One of the enlisted tells me that I looked exactly like a Kraut. An incoming German shell makes a little more rubble out of the rubble of a nearby house. This puts an end to the fun for a while.

I walk back down the cellar stairs of the ruined house being used as the command post. The room is crowded with the company headquarters personnel: the runners, the radio operators, the first sergeant, and messengers from the platoons. Captain Ritter lies on one of the bunks scattered around the room. He seems very happy; the attack was a success. He motions me over to him. "Better get some of this Jerry pork," he says. "It was cooking when we took the place." He motions to large quart-sized cans of pork meat on a table. Several of the cans are being heated on a stove. I pull out my spoon, which is always present in the breast pocket of my field jacket, and dig in to the steaming contents of a can. The pork is delicious, and fat runs down both sides of my chin. I suck the juice from the tips of my mustache and remember that in both attacks I found myself chewing the tips of my mustache. Just a nervous habit.

Captain Ritter speaks to me again. "Price, I'm saving you a bunk here where you can sleep. Say, have you seen the mess of stuff that the 99th left in this town? *Beaucoup!*" A sergeant speaks from behind me. "We found a whole field desk full of reports. Switchboards and *beaucoup* stuff." The sergeant pulls something out of his field jacket pocket. "Here, Lieutenant, have a Combat Infantry Badge courtesy of the 99th Division."

He hands me the gleaming blue and silver badge. "Why, merci, Sarg." I unbutton my field jacket top and pin the badge over my left shirt pocket. Over my shoulder I add, "Well, Captain, I'll just head back to the OP. Thanks for the chow." I clump up the steps. The cold air stings my face as I reach the top.

As I start back down the main street I see that our phone lines now stretch along the sides of the street in all directions, and that the colorful red-and-green Jerry telephone wire lies just beneath our brown-colored wire. On arriving at the observation post, Potts informs me that we now have a telephone line to the mortars. We can turn off the radio and save the battery. He reports that all is quiet to the front, but in all directions we still hear the mutter of the guns. Their bass melody never seems to end. Potts and I stay at the observation post that night, just in case of a counterattack. The night passes slowly as the cold creeps deeper into our bodies, and we stamp our feet to try to bring back some feeling. All is quiet.

The next morning I send Potts back for breakfast and examine a propaganda leaflet I picked up on the snow back at Paratroop Cross Roads. It is one of ours, dropped on the Jerry position either by our aircraft or by artillery rounds especially equipped to carry packs of leaflets instead of high explosive. On one side is a map of Germany. The extent of the advances of the Russians to the east and the Allies to the west is clearly depicted. I have a little trouble but finally translate the German text below the map:

THE RUSSIANS ARE HERE!

The above map shows the advance of the Red Army until 12 noon 24 January. In the next 24 hours the Russians will attack in the direction of Berlin. And before this pamphlet comes to you, the Russian flood will have completely engulfed Eastern Germany—the last dam is broken!

On the reverse side it says:

> THE FRONT IS BROKEN! THIS IS THE END!
> The day of the war criminals . . . stands now in front of the door!

What does the last line mean? Still, it sounds good. I hope Jerry reads them instead of using them for toilet paper as we do.

I look up from my letter to see Lieutenant Womack. He is one of the rifle platoon leaders of L Company. I have grown very attached to him, as he is extremely friendly and always wears a happy grin on his broad face. He is built like a wrestler, short and powerful.

"Hi, Price. Been looking for you. What say we don't shave until we get through the Siegfried Line?"

"Okay by me, my friend. Whiskers stay until we crack it. It's about one mile beyond tomorrow's objective, so I don't think we'll have to wait very long."

The same morning I hear the tremendous sound of firing to the east. Other units of the 26th are attacking Mürringen, the last Belgian town before the border of Germany. I wish them luck. During the next two days, I notice that the town of Büllingen begins to fill with more and more rear-area units: signalmen, engineers, and higher headquarters. This can only mean that we are going to push on soon.

And just as I predict, on the thirty-first of January, the 3d Battalion receives its attack orders. After we have been given our assignments at the company command post, I decide that it is time for me to write home. I borrow some cheap sheets of German paper from one of the runners and sit down at the German field desk to compose a letter. As usual, I feel most urgently the need to allay my mother's fears, and at the same time I curse the censorship rules that do not allow us to give details of where we are and what our plans are:

> First let me say that I haven't had any more mail since the letter saying Dad had gotten to Atlanta, so I don't know how his operation was, or anything.
>
> About the only thing that sounds good to me recently is the news of the Russian advances. Really very heartening. We have been pushing recently and ought to be in Germany pretty soon. We are beating the snow and the Germans at the same time. I am writing from a cellar in a small Belgian town that used to be German back in 1918. We took it recently and probably will leave soon. I am unwounded, safe, and healthy, though tired as hell. . . Funny how things work. A few days ago I was blasting this place with mortars, and now I'm here. We finished the meal that the Jerries had been preparing.

I am wordy today, writing five pages in all. On the back of the letter I draw a crude sketch of my face and helmet, taking extreme care to draw my mustache exactly. Underneath the sketch I write in capital letters "SEMI ANNUAL MUSTACHE REPORT!"

The next morning, the first of February, we move out at dawn. We hear reports that a large number of Germans are around Krinkelt to the northwest. Our mission is to attack into Krinkelter Forest to the north of Mürringen and seize an important crossroad in the forest. If the attack is successful, we will be in Germany. I remain attached to L Company, and L Company will lead the attack.

The company moves out to march the two kilometers to Mürringen. There is a single-file column on each side of the narrow, snow-covered road. The strange-looking white sheets on the men flap in the breeze. Potts and I march with the company

headquarters men, behind the leading platoon. We reach Mürringen without incident and see the usual signs of the recent capture of the town. It lies in complete ruins from our artillery and
mortar fire.

"You'll be sorry!" The customary taunts flow from the
men of our regiment who have captured the place. They are
happy to be spectators rather than participants. Our men grin
self-consciously; some reply with profanity. We march on east
through the ruined town, and after another kilometer cross a
small stream and enter a dark, forbidding forest. Once in the
forest, our alertness increases. The leading platoon spreads out
with flankers in the forest on each side of the road, which is
nothing more than a trail. It turns sharply north, and we are
now heading directly for our objective, about two kilometers
ahead. Our marching speed decreases as the leading scouts now
move with extreme care through the forest. I mentally note that
if we are going to hit anything, it will be soon. Our radio is
working perfectly with the mortar platoon in the rear. We are
ready.

Now it comes. Ahead of me we hear a few rifle shots, then
the sound of a German machine gun firing long bursts. One of
our automatic rifles joins in. Captain Ritter comes back to me.
"The leading squad has hit Jerries," he says. "This side of the
objective. Can you get some 81s in there?" I listen to the firing
intently. Sounds are extremely deceiving in the dense forest.
"Without observation, about all I can do is shell the area just
beyond the crossroads, Captain." I turn to Potts and tell him to
alert the mortars for a firing mission.

Captain Ritter says, "Merci" and starts back toward the
firing. I plot the coordinates of the crossroad on my map and
quickly encode them into letters, using the proper codeword. I
add about two hundred yards of range to my fire command as I

don't want to hit our attacking troops. Soon I hear my mortar rounds hitting several hundred yards ahead. Some of the bursts are louder and clearer than others. Tree bursts. A messenger from the company commander runs back to me. "Your firing's good," he says. "Keep it up!" I continue to fire area fire at the same locality. The firing ahead grows louder, and I can see riflemen rushing forward from tree to tree. I signal Potts to follow and move forward myself. The snow on the ground between the trees lightens the scene, which is now covered with the light blue smoke of the firing.

As suddenly as it began, the firing ceases. I move on to the crossroad, just in time to see our leading squads disappear into the woods across the road, which runs vertically across our route of march. On my left, about twenty yards into the woods, I see a German soldier lying dead across his light machine gun. A dead American lies nearby. A soldier standing nearby points to the American. "He got the machine gun! Rushed right at it."

Now I hear the sound of our soldiers digging in, their small folding shovels clanging loudly against the earth and rocks as they form a defensive perimeter around the crossroads. A few minutes later I hear an armored vehicle rumbling up the road behind me. It is one of our tank destroyers. It drives straight to the crossroads, stops, then backs and turns so that its gun points straight down the road coming into the crossroads from the left. I see our engineers laying mines across the same road, about fifty yards from the crossing. I am puzzled for a minute, then remember that this side road leads to Krinkelt, and if the Germans there try to break out, this will be the route they will use.

With a shock I notice that it is getting dark. Potts and I move forward across the crossroads to the platoon positions to the right front. There are several German bunkers in this area. In a few minutes it is totally dark. A squad leader, covered with mud, is moving from one German bunker to another, swearing. "These lousy holes are collapsing. Don't try to get in this one, Lieutenant; the damn thing damn near buried us." Although there is snow everywhere, the warmth of the day has melted enough snow to soften the frozen dirt into mud. "They're all leaking like sieves," the sergeant adds.

After walking from bunker to bunker for awhile, looking for a place to bed down, Potts and I are invited to sleep in the bunker of one of the rifle squads. The hole is a large one, covered with a thick layer of logs and dirt and holds about one half of the rifle squad. "Ain't got much room, but you're welcome," we are told. Potts and I squeeze into the hole. There is barely enough room for all to sit with our backs propped against the dirt walls. After eating a D-ration, which is an extremely hard chocolate bar, for our supper, Potts and I try to get some sleep. The hole stinks of dirty, smelly men and is full of smoke from the burning of the wax-coated cardboard K-ration boxes. We have found that the boxes burn extremely well, and the men often heat their rations over this blaze. Tonight they are burning them to keep warm. The roof of the hole drips water everywhere, and the water drops make a metallic clink as they strike the tops of our helmets. Finally I doze off.

Sometime during the night we are awakened by a tremendous explosion about two hundred yards to our left. The ground shakes with the concussion of one detonation after another in quick succession. We can hear yelling and small-arms fire to our left. It ends abruptly. The whole noise has lasted no longer than three minutes. Potts and I collect our gear and begin to crawl out of the hole. We find the rifle platoon leader just outside the hole. The blackness of the night is broken on our left by flickering fires, dimly visible through the trees. The platoon leader has been talking to the platoon on the left. "It's all over," he tells me. "Some Jerries tried to break out of the pocket over there. We got 'em all. Now maybe we can get some sleep." Potts and I crawl back into the hole, spread the news around, and then once again fall into a fitful sleep.

The next morning at daybreak, we walk back to the cross-road. I notice that there are several empty shell cases around the tank destroyer. The crew of the tank destroyer are cleaning their gun. They are elated. "Beautiful!" one of them says. "First they hit the mines, and then we opened up on them! They never had a chance to fire a shot!" Just behind the tank destroyer I notice two German graves, with the occupants' helmets hanging on two wooden crosses. The graves look neat and strangely geometrical. Probably killed during the earlier fighting in the breakthrough.

As we walk down the road toward the scene of the action, we see many of our soldiers milling around. The scene is ghastly. There are dead Germans everywhere. From the trees bordering the trail hang bits and pieces of clothing and human flesh. On the trail stand two smoldering German self-propelled guns. I can reconstruct the scene with no difficulty. About a platoon of German infantrymen were marching on the road into our position, one self-propelled gun just ahead of them and one following them. The self-propelled guns—we call them SPs—are heavily armored tracked vehicles with a gun protruding from their sharp, prowlike nose. The gun does not rotate from a turret like a tank gun, but can fire only to the front.

The leading SP hit a mine. Immediately our tank destroyer opened fire, scoring direct hits. The infantrymen behind must have hit the ground, and in the darkness the second SP rolled forward over the men on the road. From under the tracks of the second SP protrude the heads, torsos, and legs of a dozen German soldiers. Their bodies are black, and their clothing is still smoldering. Bluish smoke comes from the crushed chest of one. The most horrible expressions are on the burned faces of the soldiers. Their mouths are open as though they were screaming when they felt the heavy vehicle roll over them.

The ditch on either side of the trail is full of the dead. Some have had their clothing blown from their bodies by the mine explosions and the fire from the tank destroyer. Others were caught and killed by the deadly small-arms and machine-gun fire of the nearby rifle platoon. Many of the bodies are cut in half or lack a leg or an arm.

I see that our soldiers have already rifled the pockets of the dead, and I am nauseated when I see a soldier start through the breast pockets of one of the dead Germans whose body lies half under the SP. The trail is covered with the litter of war. Pieces of German equipment, rifles, gas-mask canisters, and letters and personal documents lie everywhere. I pick up one of the letters lying in the trail. It begins "Lieber Anton" and is signed by his sister. I cannot read the letter as it is written in German script, which is illegible to me. There are the usual photographs lying in the mud: proud parents, girlfriends, a kid brother in his new uniform.

I am sickened by the sights and smells and walk away. I head to the company command post, which is a shell hole about one hundred yards behind the crossroad. Already I hear soldiers beginning to refer to our location as "SP Crossroads." As good a name as any, I reflect, and there is no name given for it on any of our maps.

At the command post everyone is talking about the destruction of the German unit and the large number of enemy soldiers captured in the action. I am amazed that such activity could have taken place in such a short amount of time. Across the hood of a jeep at the command post I see a blanket covering one of our soldiers; only his brown hair and boots are visible. Captain Ritter is telling someone to notify battalion to have the body moved to the rear as soon as possible.

The next day, other units have attacked beyond us, and all is quiet. Although snow still stands on the ground, the roads and trails in the forest are now solid mud. The dirt that I have gotten all over me by sleeping in the muddy hole begins to irritate me, so I go to the command post and fill my helmet with hot water from the galvanized can in which we dip our mess gear after washing it in other cans. I borrow a mirror, soap, and a razor from someone. I prop the helmet in the snow, and hang the mirror from a tree limb.

I unsling my field glasses case and my gas mask, then take off my harness, which holds my canteen, first-aid packet, entrenching tool, trench knife, compass, pistol, and ammunition clips. Next I take off my woolen scarf, my field jacket, the brown woolen knitted sweater, my OD woolen shirt, and the long woolen underwear shirt. Under it, against my skin, I am wearing a sleeveless woolen sweater; I remove this. The sun warms my naked back, and I proceed to wash the upper part of my body. I smell better already. Using the borrowed gear, I proceed to shave the dirty stubble that covers my face, taking care not to injure the beautiful mustache. As I look in the mirror I am amazed at my pale, fleshy reflection, which seems to stand out from the dirty skin I can see through my hair and on the sides of my neck. I swish the razor around in the now-filthy water and hear someone come up behind me.

"Damn, Price!" says Lieutenant Womack. "What did you do that for? You shaved! You broke our bargain!"

"Oh God! I forgot!"

Later this day we get the news: we will attack through the Siegfried Line tomorrow. L Company, thank the Lord, will not be the leading company. Once again I feel the urge, like so many others, to write a letter home. I scrounge around for a piece of paper. "Here, lieutenant. I took it off one of those dead Krauts this morning." The soldier hands me a single sheet of extremely poor grade paper and a soiled envelope. I thank him and begin to write on the hood of the jeep. After writing the date, 3 February 1945, I write the single word "Germany," underlining it twice:

DEAREST MOTHER AND FATHER,

I wrote you a few days ago from the cellar of a small village in Belgium that our battalion captured. Since then in another push we crossed the border and are now . . .

What shall I say? Better make them feel we have already passed the Siegfried Line.

. . . well into Germany. Tough sledding behind us, and ahead of us.

I decide to write about my feet being dry and warm, then about the fact that I have still received no mail since the letter telling me that my father is home. Now, about the weather:

The weather has been a little warmer lately, enough to turn the roads to mud, and make the dugouts leak like sieves, but the snow is still here and it won't be Spring for a long time.

I write about the Russian advance, and then the urgings of my empty stomach turn my thoughts to food:

There is really nothing that you can send me, as we have all we need including cigarettes. But when you do send something make sure it's food.

Like cans of sardines, and peanut brittle or peanuts.

I end up writing about the brave soldiers with whom I am serving and express the wish that the war will end quickly. I seal and address the envelope, write "Free Mail" in place of a postage stamp, and sign my signature on the upper left hand corner, to show that I have censored my own mail—an officer's privilege.

A few minutes later, two artillery jeeps arrive, bringing the field artillery forward observer party that will accompany us in the attack tomorrow. I greet them and we start talking about the Siegfried Line. The artillerymen bring good news: some self-propelled 155-mm artillery pieces are being brought forward through the woods to place direct fire on the German pillboxes. Suddenly, we all dive for the ground, as though we are puppets and attached to the same string. At the same instant there is the tremendous whishing sound of an incoming shell, and then the explosion just on the other side of the road. I crawl behind a mound of earth and hardly notice that two others have piled on top of me in their effort to get shelter. Now another round swishes overhead and lands fifty feet beyond us. No one moves. I notice that the eyes of one of the artillerymen are glassy and open extremely wide. He stares at the ground beneath him without moving a muscle. Now a salvo of shells passes over us, all hitting in the trees about one hundred yards beyond us. We wait. There is no further shelling. From a distance I hear a riflemen in the company headquarters group. "Why doesn't somebody get those bastards?" We all get to our feet. No one is hurt.

The next morning we wait for a column of trucks to arrive. They will take us another two miles forward to a point just short of the Siegfried Line. I climb in the front seat of the two-and-a-half-ton truck loaded with riflemen. Just beyond SP Crossroads we see the remains of a German horse-drawn artillery battery that has been shelled. Dead horses lie on and by the side of the road.

Excited murmurs come from each of the trucks as they pass a dead mare, still in harness. The hind feet and body of a foal protrude from the womb of the mare. The shelling has caused her to bring forth her foal in death. I listen to the men on my truck. "Them dirty, lousy, sneakin' bastards!" A hundred feet farther on we pass two of our Sherman tanks. There are large holes in the turrets and sides from German tank fire. They have been sitting there since the sudden German breakthrough in December.

We unload from the trucks about one kilometer from the Siegfried Line and form on the road. Just ahead of us we can hear the sound of artillery fire, and the echoes of explosions rattle through the fire-breaks in the forest. We move forward a little way, stop, then move forward a little more and stop again. I am surprised that there is no incoming artillery fire. Surely Jerry knows we are using this road. Ahead I can hear German mortar rounds falling—but no artillery.

Now L Company is at the edge of the forest, and I get my first look at the Siegfried Line. First are the lines of barbed wire, then come the dragon's teeth—rounded humps designed to make a tank expose its soft belly as it attempts to roll over them. Interlaced in the teeth is more barbed wire. I can see the dragon's teeth stretching to the horizon on either side. Behind the dragon's teeth I see German pillboxes spaced about two hundred yards apart and in great depth. I am happy to see that the leading company has been making steady progress through the defenses. Through my field glasses I see that almost every pillbox has suffered direct hits from our artillery. The only defense the Germans can mount is counterfire from their own artillery. Evidently they have very little in this sector. In the distance to my right I can hear the artillery firing. The 16th Infantry, which breached the Siegfried yesterday, is mopping up in the town of Ramscheid. Our objective is Hollerath, a small town about one kilometer to our front.

The engineers have been busy. We march through the dragon's teeth, being careful to stay in the narrow lane, marked on both sides by white tape, which indicates the area that has been cleared of mines. Already a bulldozer is at work pushing dirt up over the dragon's teeth to make a roadway for our tanks and other vehicles. Ahead of us we hear sporadic small-arms fire and the explosions of grenades as the leading company continues to seize pillbox after pillbox. Maybe the intelligence reports are right: that the Germans have manned this line with cripples and second-class soldiers.

A heavy rain begins to fall. The road we are on is a great quagmire, and we sink up to our ankles even on the sides of the road. We stop long enough to slip our heads through our ponchos. Now L Company is ordered to seize the right side of Hollerath. Captain Ritter gives his orders, pointing out the location of the pillboxes on that side of Hollerath. Resistance seems very light, and I follow one of the platoons as it moves to attack a large pillbox built in the side of a steep valley. The platoon attacks from the blind side of the box. Rifle and automatic rifle fire is placed on the embrasures of the pillbox. I can hear a tremendous explosion as TNT is detonated against the steel door of the pillbox. Soon a squad of Germans are filing from the pillbox, their hands in the air.

Potts and I move forward and enter the pillbox. I am amazed at the ingenuity of its construction. Inside there are tiers of bunks—enough for a whole platoon—and even a built-in bathroom. Every entrance has double baffles made of heavy steel, as do the machine-gun embrasures. The pillbox stinks of stale sweat and smoke and the fumes of high explosives. I look out the main machine-gun firing slit. From it I have a beautiful view of the valley, but there is no possibility that the Germans could have fired up on the plateau over which we advanced. It becomes apparent that every pillbox depends on the fires of other pill-boxes to protect its blind spots. Once one fortification is cap-tured, you have knocked a hole in the defenses of several others.

It is rapidly growing dark. Over our radio, we hear that our mortars are now in a position behind us, and Potts and I go up above the pillbox to begin registering defensive fires. The occa-sional bursts of small-arms fire in the town have ceased. I find that Hollerath is almost surrounded on the south and east by an extremely deep valley and begin to understand why it was so lightly defended. Jerry would have a hard time supplying it from the east. I begin to plot and fire white phosphorous rounds in a semicircle around our position until I am satisfied that I can bring fire on any of the danger areas.

Potts and I walk back up the hill in the dark to the road leading into the town. We stumble through deep ruts filled with water in the road, and in some low places the entire roadbed is covered with water. We also stumble over boxes and pieces of equipment lying in the road. I can see that about half of the houses are in ruins from our artillery fire. About half way down the main street we find a house with its roof still standing, and I tell Potts to report our location to the command post and then return.

I enter the living room of the house alone. There are black-out curtains on the windows, and so, using my flashlight, I search for a candle. Finding one in a drawer, I light it and place it in the center of a table. Outside the night is quiet. I begin to examine some books lying on the floor. One is a small volume of Goethe's *Faust*. I sink into a chair and begin trying to read it. But I find that I am tired and can scarcely keep my eyes open. I lie down on a couch and fall asleep. I am instantly awakened

when Potts enters the room. Seeing who it is, I wish him pleasant dreams, and go right back to sleep.

At the company command post the next day, I get the wonderful news that we are being relieved by the 99th Division, and
that we, wonder of wonders, will go back into a rest area in
Belgium. During the morning we stand in the doorways of the
houses and watch the double file of infantrymen from the 99th
stream through the town, moving forward to take over the positions of our men. Their black-and-white checkerboard shoulder
patches stand out against the drab color of their field jackets.
Our men greet them with the usual cry of "You'll be sorry!"
Some have more uncomplimentary things to say. Most of the
men look like new replacements, and I noticed that they do not
take their eyes off the mud and water in which they are walking. Our jibes die away. The 99th caught hell during the Bulge.

In the middle of the afternoon we form in the muddy main
street and begin to march out of Hollerath to the rear. There
are the usual delays, halts, and starts, and hours later we reach
the place where we are to entruck. We have marched back
through the Siegfried Line and are about one kilometer beyond
it. Darkness falls as we stand around the roadside waiting for our
trucks, which have been shuttling troops back into Belgium. It
is bitterly cold, and a heavy wind is blowing.

Just before dark I noticed a side road coming into our main
road. I decide to walk down this side road. I will be able to hear
our trucks when they arrive. The road I am walking on goes
through a patch of heavy forest and turns sharply across a small
open field. There is sufficient light in the sky reflected on the
snow to see about ten or fifteen yards. As I walk through the
field, I begin to notice objects in the field to my left. I leave the
road and walk toward them.

As I come closer I can make out a man on the ground—a

German. He holds both arms out toward me above his body. I am shocked and draw back. Now I see on each side of him other Germans. As far as I can see in all directions there are others. Dead Germans, half-uncovered by the melting snows, in every conceivable position. There are dozens of bodies, all laid out in neat rows. I shiver, more from the eerie sight than from the cold. I slowly walk along the front row of bodies. Some lie on their backs with their legs elevated, some hold their arms up, many hold their heads up off the ground in their frozen positions and seem to be staring at me. It seems that everyone is frozen into the position he held when he was killed. Many are squatting or sitting.

As my night vision improves, it dawns on me that the entire small field is covered with these bodies. It is a German collection point for the dead killed during the breakthrough fighting. I feel a strong desire to run and walk hastily back through the trees to the main road. I say nothing about my discovery, and soon our trucks arrive.

We drive through the night, with only the tiny blackout lights to guide us. I fall asleep several times, only to be awakened as the truck lurches through a hole in the road. We drive back through Krinkelter Forest, and then through several small towns standing in ruins, and finally arrive in the familiar town of Butgenbach, the site of Colonel Corley's command post during our defense. Stiffly we crawl from our trucks and move into some of the less-damaged houses. We are grateful that there is hot chow waiting for us, and then we all find a space on the floors of the houses and fall asleep.

Early the next morning everyone is talking and laughing. The relief of being in the rear manifests itself in jokes and boisterous behavior. Looking around, I discover that almost all the snow has melted and decide to rid myself of the German snow trousers I have been wearing. I take them off and leave them hanging on a hook on the back of a door. Many of the riflemen in the room joke about my "Jerry britches"; others tell me how much they wished that they had a pair during the fighting in the snow. Later in the morning our trucks arrive, and we gladly mount the vehicles, which are taking us back deeper into Belgium for the long-awaited rest.

WAITING ON THE RIVER

The deeper our trucks drive back into Belgium, the more green and beautiful the scenery becomes. As we drive through the shell-pocked villages, I see an occasional dead German lying in the roadside ditch—now revealed by the melting snow. Later in the day we arrive at the large Belgian town where our entire regiment is to be billeted.

The hospitality of the Belgian people is magnificent. I find myself billeted in a Belgian home with about twelve men. It is almost comical to watch the men sitting on the living room floor watching the family go about its daily pursuits. Like most Belgian families, this one consists of a grandmother, husband and wife, and children of various ages. The family insists that I sleep on a bed, although I tell them I would be just as comfortable sleeping on the floor with the other soldiers, and the housewife insists that she be allowed to do our washing for us. None of us speaks French well enough to tell her that we can do it ourselves.

The next morning we are pleased to not hear shellfire in the distance. The silence is wonderful. We share our rations with the Belgian family, and after breakfast, I check in with the M Company command post and then take a long jeep drive with another officer to the Belgian town of Spa. Here, in a picturesque small hotel near the edge of town, we order our lunch. Although I suspect that the fried steak we are eating is horse, I find the meal delicious. We buy several glasses of Cognac to top off the repast.

Our stay in Belgium ends abruptly two days later, when we are alerted to a move back up into the Aachen sector of Germany. We are told that we will be used in forcing a crossing over the Roer River, the next major barrier inside of Germany. This rather dashes our spirits, but we have enjoyed our interlude. Before we load onto the trucks, the order is passed to everyone to take off our 1st Division shoulder patches, and the markings on the bumpers of all of our vehicles are covered with mud or tape to hide the identification of our unit.

Our route to the north takes us through the town of Eupen, Belgium, and I remember the brick factory here, where I was assigned to the 1st Division. Soon our column is heading into the outskirts of Aachen, Germany, and I am amazed at the absolute destruction of the city. We drive through block after block of nothing but rubble, and then, turning south, our column moves into the foreboding darkness of Hurtgen Forest. A silence falls over the men, many of whom fought here in November. We climb steadily for miles along muddy roads that are bordered with thick fir and pine trees. The farther we go toward the eastern edge of the forest, the deeper the mud becomes. Finally, we leave the somewhat improved main road near Grosshau and turn back into the depths of the forest for another mile.

The mud is incredible. The jeep on which I am riding sinks deeper and deeper into the oozing road. The problem is made worse by the heavy trucks ahead of us, which have cut two deep ruts into the mud. At several points the mud is so high it sloshes onto the floor of the jeep, and I marvel at the power of our vehicle when it is in four-wheel drive. Just when the road becomes impassible, I see the men dismounting from the trucks ahead of us. We are here.

I look around and find that M Company is to occupy a small clearing in the forest, which extends on both sides of the muddy road. For the past hour we have heard the mutter of artillery in all directions and therefore get to work with a will in constructing our sleeping holes. There is plenty of wood for overhead cover, and soon the area is dotted with dirt-covered mounds. This is my first opportunity to spend any length of time with the mortar platoon. Now, soldiers who were just voices on the radio or telephone begin to take on personalities.

After we have been in the forest about two days, we receive word that the Germans have somehow damaged the dams at the head of the Roer River to such an extent that the river is several feet higher than usual. We will wait here until the river subsides enough for an assault crossing. Although most soldiers are jubilant on hearing this news, some of the officers point out that this means the Germans will have much more time to perfect their defenses across the Roer.

On the 12th of February I write home:

Now undergoing one of those hurry up and wait jobs. You would be surprised to know that when not fighting, our Infantry men are the most idle people in the world. When they have built shelter, and cleaned weapons, there is nothing more to do, and they just settle down to bull shooting, and getting on each other's nerves. . . . There are a few left from Africa, a few more from Sicily, and a smattering from D-day France. I have a few experiences to resift myself, and will have more, I'm afraid. Well, the news continues good, the snow is gone, and for three days it has rained. We have a fairly waterproof dugout here, and are getting wonderful chow. Our kitchens are right with us here, instead of being anywhere from 5 to 25 miles behind us as usual. Another advantage, eating chow in daylight, instead of waiting for dark so that Jerry can't see you eating. Really nice not to have to depend on nose and tongue to tell the menu.

We are four miles from the Roer River, and although we are in range of German artillery, Lieutenant Ciccone decides to erect his large command-post tent. I watch the soldiers put up the tent, and after it is up, I examine it with curiosity. The top of the tent is full of shell-fragment holes, and both the top and sides are scorched in many places. Nevertheless, it becomes the focal point for the platoon, and the folding tables and chairs in it are soon filled with men writing letters and playing cards.

The day after writing my first letter from this tent, we see our first German jet fighter aircraft. First we hear the bark of distant antiaircraft guns and, looking up in the sky, see the black puffs of smoke as the antiaircraft shells burst, but we can not see the target. Finally, someone spots it. "Look! Way up above the bursts! A Jerry plane!" We focus our eyes on the speck high above us. The German plane, even at its unbelievable altitude, seems to be moving tremendously fast. And it appears to be at least a mile higher than the shells bursting below it. Now from several directions we see our own fighter planes approaching at extreme altitude, but the Jerry plane mocks their efforts by flying at least twice as fast as our propeller-driven fighters.

All over the area we hear units beginning to fire up at the Jerry. Now some of our men are hastily setting up our .50-caliber machine gun on its high tripod. Soon the rapid firing of this machine gun adds to the noise of the other guns. The sky is filled with tracers. I can't help but think that this is ridiculous, as no weapon we have can reach the altitude of that enemy fighter. But everyone else seems to think that this is great sport. Suddenly, we hear a whistle coming toward us and then there is a small explosion in the center of our field. A soldier curses and drops to the ground, holding his thigh. I rush over and discover that he has a fragment of an explosive shell, probably fired by one of our fighter planes above, in his leg. He is assisted to the nearby medical officer's tent, and this incident puts an end to the fun. A few minutes later, we see the German fighter lazily turn and proceed back toward his own lines.

To occupy ourselves, the platoon engages in a lot of mortar drill, and I am amazed to find how proficient the old hands are at setting up the mortars. The machine-gun platoons also conduct drills, and, on a dare, I prove that I can pick up one of the water-cooled heavy machine guns, tripod, water, and all, and run with it for fifty yards. This load is normally carried by two men. I win my bet.

Hikes are prescribed, and the platoon makes long marches through the firebreaks and trails in the forest. We often encounter signs of the fighting of last November. On one occasion we find the legless body of a German soldier. A great deal of rusting and rotting German and American equipment is discovered in the dank and dreary forest. On St. Valentine's Day, the fourteenth, I write my parents, describing our worst foe of the present—mud:

> I believe I have told you that the snow is gone, but still there are the after effects. I find that mud is as bad as snow. You should be quite amazed if you could see me now. I am as stout as ever, but my mustache has quite a point at each extremity. In fact, I have the second longest in the company. I don't suppose you could stand me around very long, though, as our

hands are black and cracked, and rough; our hair matted, and though we all shave at least once every three days when in an assembly area like this, our faces get dirty fast. It all comes from living in such proximity to the ground.

Not liking to be idle, I find myself composing a poem about the mortar platoon. The regimental special service officer, who publishes a humorous, nine-page mimeograph newspaper called the *Spade* (the spade is our regimental insignia), hears of the poem and asks me for a copy of it. I oblige. Publishing is not big business in an infantry regiment, and the sheet seems to come out only when we are in rest periods or in assembly areas. Nevertheless, we enjoy reading it. At the top of the front page are two spades, and at the bottom it always reads, "DESTROY* DO NOT LET FALL INTO ENEMY HANDS." My poem, "Ciccone's 'Lads,'" is published on the twenty-fourth of February, the day before we cross the Roer.

Each evening all of the mail written during the day is piled on a table in the tent. Each officer takes a handful of the letters and begins the chore of censoring. Following an unwritten law, we take the letters at random and no soldier is to know which officer has censored his mail. I find the letters extremely dull for the most part. This is not the fault of the soldiers but due to the restrictions against writing of our locations and activities. In addition, most of the letters deal with family matters, which mean nothing to anyone but the writer and recipient. Only rarely do we have to cut out from a letter.

I greatly appreciate the officers and men of the mortar platoon. Lieutenant Ciccone refers to himself as the "master" and always answers the phone with that word. He rules the platoon with an iron hand when there is business to be done but displays a marvelous sense of humor when relaxing with his "lads." The other two second lieutenant forward observers,

George Nestor and Overton Hubbard, are now great pals of mine. Hubbard attended the Virginia Military Institute and rags me constantly about my alma mater, the Citadel. S.Sgt. Thomas Boyle is a highly intelligent, clean-cut young man, and I am delighted to hear that he is being considered for a battlefield commission.

My first radio operator, Jimmy Higgins, has a reputation for neatness and cleanliness. The lads kid him about his fastidiousness and often call him "Romeo" Higgins. Fred Riebel, the other radio operator, usually works with George Nestor. He is an unusually well read and profound person, and I often discuss philosophy with him far into the night. Both Potts and Riebel have families at home, about whom they never cease to talk. In fact, a high percentage of the officers and noncommissioned officers in the platoon are married. Being a bachelor, I never cease to be amazed that these married men can go about their business in combat in such a courageous fashion, knowing all the while that their death will leave a family without support. Allie Potts often speaks of his work as a flight test engineer before coming into the infantry. I find myself becoming fonder and fonder of this clear-eyed, bright young man from Alabama.

Father Bracken is as interesting as ever and will stop anyone to describe "Seemosaye," a mythical land he has invented. He loves to talk about this place of beauty and absence of aggravation. I can tell that he is putting into words his own longing to be done with war. He sits in the tent at night for hours telling us of "that faraway land where there is no mail censorship" or "that wonderful place that has never heard of rain." In Seemosaye, he says, "they don't even know what a machine gun is."

I often ponder this utopia, and one day I decide to write a poem for Father. One of the soldiers has picked up a German portable typewriter in the ruins of a house, and he lends it to me whenever I want to type. I write out a longhand draft, make a few corrections, and then type two copies so that I can keep one for myself.

SEEMOSAYE

Dedicated to the discoverer of Seemosaye, James J. Bracken.

PROLOGUE

I spoke one night to a soldier,
And heard what he had to say.
And the tale he told was astounding,
'Twas the tale of Seemosaye.

When first he started to tell me,
The story seemed quite remote,
And I gave him scant attention,
For he spoke as if by rote.

But gradually all of my thoughts
Began to fade away,
As I heard of incredible beauty—
The place called Seemosaye.

I missed his whole beginning
And cursed my wand'ring mind,
For I didn't know if he made it up
Or had really made the find.

But now with rapt attention
I heard his tale unfold,
And of this land of Seemosaye,
Where streets are paved with gold.

THE TALE OF SEEMOSAYE

In Seemosaye, the soldier said, the land is green and bright,
The people sing throughout the day, and often through the
* night.*
The children come without the pain that all our wives do fear,
And all the seasons come to one; it's Spring throughout the
* year.*
The thought of crime's unheard of, and they have no word for
* war.*
Instead, their language speaks of love, of laughs, of life, of
* lore.*
They have a lot of adjectives that we have never heard;
They cannot speak unless there is a smile with every word.
The road that leads to Seemosaye is lined with plants and trees,
And from them comes a music when there is a gentle breeze.
The road is easy to the feet, its curves are gentle, too,
There are no milestones on the way for that would never do.
Those are nice things about the road, and some are better still.
For instance, though it's in the hills, you never walk uphill.
And if your feet are weary, there is no harsh dismay;
A little stream is flowing there to wash the pain away.
There is no wall at Seemosaye; there is no barring gate,
Just homes and halls and rooftops of burnished golden plate.
The streets are wide and twisting so a man can never say
That he was routed quickly through the streets of Seemosaye.
Instead, it is more likely that he stopped at every door,
And stayed a happy day or two, or maybe three or four.
There is no work in Seemosaye; the farming—it is play.
The cattle graze and reproduce—it seems to work that way.
There are no fences round the fields, for cattle never stray,
And eggs there are aplenty, for even roosters lay.
And once the seed is planted, for duties they have few;

The ground is fertilizer, and for water there is dew.
I think that I forgot to mention that it never rains,
For rain makes mud, and mud is nasty, which I think explains.
The people live a happy life, I'm sure that you must see,
For selfishness is never here, for everyone is free.
I know you wonder how they die in this green paradise,
I know but little on that score; 'twill have to you suffice.
When comes the time that one grows old, as we must all one
*   day,*
The person goes into the hills, the hills of Seemosaye.

> EPILOGUE
> *I wish that I were there right now,*
> *The poet soldier said.*
> *In that fair land where there's no cause*
> *An angry tear to shed.*
>
> *And if I keep on roaming,*
> *I'm sure someday I'll find*
> *That paradise of Seemosaye,*
> *That's always on my mind.*

I finish writing the poem on the nineteenth of February. Father Bracken, delighted with my effort, hastens to point out that to tell the entire story of Seemosaye would require a book of poetry. "Yes, Father" is my only reply. During this period we receive the Stars and Stripes every day, and we all take a great interest in the progress of the war, including the assault on the Philippines. Mail arrives regularly, and I write letters every day.

The problem of the muddy roads never ends. Every day a platoon of men are sent to some part of the forest road network to work with the engineers on corduroying the roads. I take my turn as officer-in-charge of this work and am amazed at the mile after mile of logs sunk into the mud to provide a hard surface. On one occasion I find myself at the point where the main road emerges from the forest and runs downhill to the Roer River. I note the large sign nailed to a tree: Caution! Road Beyond This Point Shelled Frequently.

Around the twentieth of February rumors of impending movement are borne out by headquarters. We are issued maps of the area just on the other side of the Roer; the known German trenches, pillboxes, and minefields are marked in bold red ink. Our artillery observation aircraft begin to take company and battalion officers up for flights overlooking the German positions. We have equipment checks every day, and finally, on the twenty-fourth, we are assembled at M Company headquarters to receive the attack order. Captain Nechey tells us that we will cross the next day near the town of Niderau over bridges to be thrown over the river by the 8th Division. We will follow 8th Division units across and then swing to the south. We are greatly relieved to hear that we will not have to force the crossing of the Roer.

Lieutenants Nestor, Hubbard, and I are soon at work copying page after page of artillery concentration coordinates in our notebooks, which we will later mark on our maps. Each set of coordinates has its own letter and number, and thus, instead of sending back for fire on a road junction located at map coordinates 10623488, we can merely call for fire on concentration Mike One. We note that the artillery concentrations extend far across the map to the west, an indication that the higher headquarters believes we will be able to move fast once we cross. Once again I am attached to Captain Ritter's L Company for the attack.

The next morning I write my last letter from Hurtgen Forest just prior to our departure. The sound of heavy artillery fire has filled the air since early morning. The guns roar endlessly, and occasionally German shells fall in the forest near our area. As usual, my letter does not mention the impending attack but does reveal my gloom:

DEAREST MOTHER,

I received so many letters from you last night that I couldn't help but be overwhelmed by your devotion. . . . There were eleven from you. They dated from about 17 Nov. to Jan. 3 and I guess that's all of the back mail.

But those letters from you revealed many things. At first, there was the optimism that you seemed to feel shortly after I left, then the period when your spirit just about gave out due to the years of loneliness, and this continued for about a week or more, and then those letters from dad starting to hint, and your letters acted hopeful, although you were afraid to believe what you read, and then those glad, unbelievably happy letters telling of Dad's return, and then the news of Hick's pending rotation. Why, it was like reading a novel of fiction that turns out to be the truth.

Yes, it was about time you got a break, and I can't help but believe that it was due to your own goodness—your constant letter writing, prayers, and thoughts that brought you your own reward. . . . How did I ever get a mother who stands so high above the crowd? I am indeed fortunate . . .

I am happy. . . . Then, too, I am healthy, my diarrhea is gone, or did you know about that, and I am thrilled that the weather is up a few degrees. Bitter, but warmer. I am not depressed, rather, honored to be able to be in on this thing. . . . I am not cowardly, I found that out many weeks ago. So you see, all I have to do is go when we must, rest when I can, and think of the beautiful future.

The envelope is sealed and in the hands of our mail clerk. It takes but a few minutes to roll up my sleeping bag and sling and buckle all of my assorted equipment. Now I stand by the road, with hundreds of others, waiting for the signal to move out.

6 ☆

ROER TO THE RHINE

We move by truck a few kilometers. At the top of the ridge overlooking the Roer River, I see the sign that warns that the road ahead is frequently shelled. The soldiers joke about this as we hear the roar of artillery, both German and ours, in all directions. A military policeman of the 1st Division, standing in a deep foxhole, with only the top of his helmet and his hands visible, is directing traffic at the point where the forest ends. I do not blame him for his precautions. The road down toward the ruined village of Gey is full of shell holes, so we dismount from the trucks to proceed on foot.

We continue to march through mud to the north until we are almost opposite the town of Niderau, which lies just on the far bank of the Roer. Although German artillery shells drop around us with increasing frequency, the long column does not halt, and soon it is our turn to march across a floating footbridge. Only a few men are allowed on the bridge at a time. We instinctively pick up our speed as we cross it. I am amazed at the width of the river and the rapidity with which the brown, muddy water swirls beneath us.

At the far end of the bridge we can look down at an old bridge abutment, part of a bridge that has been blown. Just below me, I see the body of one of our soldiers. The top of his head is missing, and pinkish-white glistening brain matter is splashed on the stone where he lies. One of his arms points to the east, and he seems to say, "Welcome to the east bank of the Roer." I wrench my eyes from this sight. Ahead I see that the column is turning to the right and moving south along the riverbank.

As we march on, the roar of battle to our front, left, and rear grows in intensity. We walk extremely close to the riverbank and soon make out the type of defenses the Germans prepared. The riverbank is covered with antipersonnel mines, usually fastened to steel stakes driven in the ground. Barbed-wire entanglements are everywhere. We thank our lucky stars that we did not have to force a crossing at this point. The houses we pass stand in ruins from the continual artillery fire to which they have been subjected during the past few weeks, especially the preattack barrages.

We halt in the town of Kreuzau, about one mile south of our crossing point. The men seek shelter in the ruined houses of the town, and soon darkness falls. As we await further orders, we can hear the sound of battle going on to the south and southeast of us, as other units continue to roll the German river defenses back from the crossing point. About midnight, the order is passed from house to house to move out. We form in the street, and L Company takes up its march again. I notice that we have taken the road that leads away from the river toward the town of Drove. As there is no sound of firing from the direction we are marching, we assume that the town has been cleared of the enemy.

After a two-mile march, we pass the first houses of the town. Darkness hides the sights of the recent combat here, and we move on into the center of the town. We are ordered not to go in the houses but to remain on the street for further orders. Soon the word is passed back for me to go forward and find the company commander. Potts and I move up the main street and then to the right on a road that leads out of the town to the south. Nowhere have we seen any sign of the unit that captured Drove, and I imagine that they are either outposting the town or in the houses.

I find Captain Ritter, who is briefing his platoon leaders on his new orders, in a large house that has been hastily blacked out. He tells us that battalion has ordered L Company to make a surprise attack to seize Boich, an important town about one mile to the southwest of us and back toward the river. Battalion feels that one company should be able to do the job, as the German defenses are probably concentrated on the river side of the town. We will be attacking them from their right rear, and, as in the case of Büllingen, coming in through the back door, so to speak. Captain Ritter says that there will be no artillery preparation. His plan of attack unfolds: one platoon will attack straight down the main road to Boich, with tanks accompanying the infantrymen; the other leading platoon will be to the left of the road, following a stream that runs in a valley from Drove to Boich.

"No one is to go to the right of the road to Boich!" he declares. "*Beaucoup* mines in the fields to the right of the road! Jerry expects our attack to come across those fields and has really mined the place, Everybody got that?" There is a mur-

mur of assent. I watch my buddy, Lieutenant Womack, whose eyes glitter in the light of the flashlights. He actually looks like he is enjoying himself. Captain Ritter makes further assignments of the heavy-machine-gun platoon and tells the attached tank platoon leader to keep one tank back with the command group.

"Price, you stay close to me. Okay?"

"Yes, sir."

"Merci." As usual it comes out "mercy."

I study Captain Ritter's face. How many times has this veteran company commander issued an attack order like this? His wool knit cap is tilted back on his head, and he seems no more concerned than he would be if he were conducting a training exercise in the States. He concludes by stating that the attack will be launched at dawn, "so that we can see what we're doing," and adds that he is going to be at the last house on the edge of town on the road to Boich when the attack begins.

When we are dismissed, Womack chats with me for a moment. He grins as he says, "I've got that funny *feeling,* Price."

"So have I," I reply. A company attack from one direction instead of simultaneously hitting the town with another company from another direction does not sound too promising. I follow Captain Ritter to the last house on the left at the edge of town. All is silent ahead of us. There is a mutter of artillery to the south, but the only sounds we hear are the clatter of gear as units move about and the soft sound our rubber-soled combat boots make on the pavement. Soon we are eating breakfast from our rations and waiting for dawn. One of the runners magically appears with hot coffee, which he has somehow managed to make. I gratefully accept a canteen cup half full, then study my map, which is in a plastic map case.

As the first light begins to appear in the east, I hear the clumping and rattling of a platoon moving past the house, heading out of town. It is the platoon that will attack on the right along the road. I follow Captain Ritter out of the house, and as we stand in a small orchard just in front of it, I unbutton my field jacket and slip the map case inside, where it will be out of my way. As I refasten my jacket, one of our tanks rumbles forward into the orchard, taking up a position a few yards from the house.

Now it is dawn. Visibility improves rapidly, and in a few minutes the ground haze, which clings to the valley on the left, is burned away. I begin a study of the terrain through my field glasses. I can see our platoon of riflemen on the main road, creeping cautiously forward, and I can make out the tanks following the platoon. To my left I can see nothing of the platoon in the valley, as they have some cover in the stream bed and woods on the far side of the valley. The troops on the tree-lined road reach a bend in the road, which turns slightly to the left and then heads directly for Boich. So far so good! Then the show begins.

Far ahead I hear the sudden staccato of a machine gun, instantly followed by rifle and automatic-rifle fire. To the left I can hear a German machine gun firing. It seems to come from across the valley. I study the hillside on the left with my glasses and make out a large barn that appears to be full of hay. As I watch, I believe I can hear and see the muzzle blasts of a machine gun. I run over to the tank and direct the attention of the tank commander to the barn. It is almost a kilometer away but within the range of the tank gun. In a few seconds the tank commander has fired his first round, an armor-piercing round, at the target. He quickly reloads with a high-explosive shell and pumps another round toward the target. I am standing to the left front of the tank, and the two explosions of the tank gun almost lift my head from my shoulders. The concussion is terrific.

Through my glasses I see the entire barn burst into a bright yellow flame. If there was a machine gunner there, he is now out of business. As I watch the barn burn and search the hillside near it for another target, there is a sudden explosion on the tank beside me. Hissing shell fragments zip through the air in all directions. I run to the tank and see that a shell has struck the turret of the tank just in front of the hatch in which the tank commander was standing. He is horribly wounded. The majority of the shell fragments went in the direction of the first sergeant of L Company, who was standing on the other side of the tank. He is riddled with tiny splinters of steel. In a matter of seconds the wounded first sergeant is being carried to the rear by our medics, and the tank quickly starts its motor and moves back into the town to gain the protection of the houses.

Captain Ritter seems to never take his eyes away from the men advancing to our front. He signals me to follow him and moves out down the road leading to Boich. We do not have time to wonder where the shell that struck the tank came from. I follow Ritter and his runners, staying about fifteen yards behind him. At first we walk down the center of the road. After walking about one hundred yards, I see a startling sight to our left rear on the wooded hillside overlooking Drove. One after another, several German self-propelled guns stick their ugly snouts from the edge of the wooded ridge. I call to Captain Ritter, and he too stares at the interlopers. While we watch, the Jerry guns begin firing on the town we have just left.

Now all hell breaks loose. Behind the German armored vehicles I can see Jerry infantrymen moving in the attack. Some of them see us on the road and direct the fire of their machine guns at us. One of the self-propelled guns turns and opens fire on our small group. As we dive into the ditch at the left side of our road, German mortar rounds begin to land near our position.

Captain Ritter screams above the sound of the bullets cracking above us and the explosions of the shells. "Come on! Let's get up with the Company! There's nothing we can do here!"

Ritter sets the example and begins dashing up the road toward his attacking troops. As Potts and I run after him, I cannot help but think of the horror that will ensue if the Germans cut the road behind us and catch L Company between two fires. As mortar shells continue to strike the road and fields on both sides of the road, Potts and I dive into the ditch on the right side of the road. Just as I hit the ground, I remember that this is the side of the road that is heavily mined. To hell with that. I'll risk the mines for the safety of the ditch any day.

I cast a quick glance behind me. It looks like the German self-propelled guns are moving in the direction of the road behind us. All of my thoughts go now to the precious map I am carrying. If the Germans capture the map, they will have all of our concentrations for miles ahead and can easily determine our whole regimental plan of attack. I must bury the map! While Potts watches, I scrape a hole in the dirt and place my map case in it. I cover the hole with dirt and leaves, hastily spreading the material around until it looks natural. Then, seeing that Captain Ritter has gotten far ahead of me, I jump to my feet and begin rushing down the ditch on the mined side of the road.

I glance back and see that Potts is about five yards behind me. Suddenly there is a terrific explosion about ten yards to the right of Potts. We hit the ground briefly, then once again we are up and running. Moments later, I feel myself being thrown forward by an enormous blast directly behind me, and at the same time I hear the sound of the explosion. At the same instant I feel something strike my right leg just behind the knee. At first I feel no pain, and I believe that once again a fragment has struck me but not penetrated the skin. I realize that I have been thrown out on the paved road, and I look back to see that Potts is down in the ditch. He must have been much closer to the explosion.

I call back to him, "Potts! Are you all right!"

"Lordy, that was a close one! Right between us!"

Now I feel the burning pain behind my knee and feel a trickle of something warm running down my leg. "Something hit me!" I call back. "Come on, let's move out of here!" I am still worried about the Germans to our rear. I get to my feet and discover I can walk without difficulty, and so we begin to run up the road again. This time, we stay out of the ditch on the right. The thought strikes me that I may have stepped on a German "Schuh" mine, and that my speed was the only thing that caused it not to explode under my foot.

We catch up with members of the command group, who are huddled on the road, watching the attack to our front. A German machine gun is firing steadily down the road from what appears to be a bunker just at the outskirts of town. A medic drops back along the road to me and asks me if I am hit. I tell him to look at my leg, and he soon is busy at his work, squatting beside me on the road, seemingly oblivious to the furious fire fight to our front. He slits my trouser leg about ten inches, then cuts a slit in my long underwear. "Yep! They got you right behind the knee, Lieutenant. Not bad though. I'll patch you up." He calmly tells me that one of the platoon leaders has been wounded over on the left. I wonder where he gets his information. These medics seem to have a fantastic grapevine.

While he is putting on a first-aid dressing, I look up to see Lieutenant Womack walking calmly down the road. His face is white, and he holds one arm in his other arm. I see blood staining his field jacket. He stops and grins when he recognizes me. "Hey, Price, I've got the million dollar wound!" He moves on back down the road. I look back and see that the German attack on Drove has evidently been driven off, as all is quiet in that direction.

"Look out for Krauts in those woods to your right," I warn him.

"Take care of yourself," he calls back over his shoulder to me.

The medic finishes with me. "You'll be okay, Lieutenant. Want to go back to the medics?" I think for a moment. Two platoon leaders and one first sergeant down, and the attack still going on. "No, I'm okay. Thanks." I turn back to Potts and find that the explosion has neatly severed the antenna of the radio he carries on his back. Potts shows me where fragments have torn his clothing, but miraculously he is untouched.

Captain Ritter asks me how my leg is and then says he wants artillery fire on the ridge to the left of the town. I walk with a slight limp, but otherwise I am in fine shape. I move up to the artillery forward observer and repeat Captain Ritter's request. We study his map, and I regret that I buried mine. As my radio is out of commission, the artillery officer uses his set, and soon the battery volleys of shells begin to fall on the desired spot. This heavy fire seems to end the resistance to our front.

Now ahead of me I see the tanks have moved forward and are firing into the houses on the edge of the town. Each round goes through several houses before exploding, and I feel that this will certainly stop any resistance in the houses of the town. Soon the tanks stop firing, and I can see German soldiers running from my left to the main road with their hands in the air. The riflemen are flushing them out of their holes; all resistance seems to have been broken. Within moments a stream of Jerries is passing me, trotting to the rear.

Earlier, just as the artillery fire began to fall, I picked up an American submachine gun, called a "grease gun" because of its short, fat barrel. It belonged to a wounded soldier. Now I keep this weapon pointed toward the prisoners as they pass, shouting for those who do not have their hands on their heads to put them there. The prisoners are dirty and ragged-looking, and I can see that some are in a state of shock from the intense artillery fire. Blood streams down several faces. A lone rifleman accompanies each group of twenty or thirty prisoners.

Now we move farther up the road toward the town. I see a medic working on one of our wounded in the ditch to the right. The wounded man is unconscious, and the medic has exposed his back. Almost in the center of his back is a bullet hole, through which I can hear air being sucked and expelled. The medic begins to wrap a first-aid dressing around the poor lad, and he tells me that the man received his wound while charging a German machine gun in the small concrete bunker just ahead of me. "He got the machine gun," the medic adds.

As we enter the town, I can hear an occasional shot fired ahead of us as the riflemen continue to mop up the town. Captain Ritter establishes his command post in the cellar of a ruined house in the middle of the remains of the town. He is soon busy organizing the defense of the town, while I get to work interrogating prisoners. I learn that a paratroop unit was ordered to counterattack the town of Drove at dawn, just as we launched our attack from Drove to Boich. Most of the prisoners in the town are paratroopers. They are a tough bunch. One tells me that we never would have taken the town if we had attacked from the direction of the river as they had expected.

I walk out of the cellar onto the main street of the village. Across the street I see a group of paratroopers standing in a doorway under guard. I walk over and address a German sergeant. He, and the whole group, come to a half-hearted attention, and I see sneers on their faces. I ask for his unit, and he refuses to answer. I turn to another; he gives me his rank, name, and service number, but nothing else. I secretly reflect that they are good soldiers. The group does not relax until I move away. Shortly after, I see them marched off out of town.

I decide that I should try to retrieve my map case, and I hitch a ride with an ambulance driving back to Drove. I am amazed at how far it is from the town we have captured back to our jump-off town. It is difficult to remember where I was when I buried the case, but I dismount from the ambulance at the approximate spot and begin my search, careful to stand on the paved road and not step down into the ditch. I examine the ditch for about fifty yards in both directions but find no clue to the whereabouts of my map case. Finally, I give up and hitch a ride back into Boich with an armored half-tracked vehicle. As we drive back along the road to Boich, I see an American soldier lying in the ditch. He was not there when I passed that spot a few minutes earlier. I tell the driver to stop, and I examine him. The lad is dead. I report this at the company command post, and litter bearers are sent out to retrieve him.

By now my leg is throbbing and a little painful. I crawl into a bunk, occupied that morning by the German defenders, and try to get some rest. Captain Ritter asks me if I want to examine the German defenses with him, but I decline on the grounds that I want to rest my leg. He leaves the cellar, and then I realize that I have not set up an observation post. I find Potts, and together we locate a house that has part of its roof and second story intact. Once again I take up my vigil, observing to the east. I see nothing moving on the long ridge that overlooks the town. The same evening, another unit passes through our lines and attacks farther to the east, and the next morning we find ourselves in the rear again. This leapfrogging of units forward in the attack is paying off. The Germans never are given time to recover from one attack before another is launched.

The next morning I decide that things are quiet enough for me to find a medic and have him look at my leg. Captain Ritter tells me that the battalion aid station is in a little town back on the Roer River to the west of us. He lets me have his jeep and driver to take me back. The jeep driver asks me if I can man the machine gun, which is mounted on a steel rod between the front seats of the jeep. He says that there are possible snipers in the fields west of our town. I agree, and we make the trip with me standing behind the .30-caliber machine gun, loaded and ready to fire. Although we see no enemy on our drive, I am impressed with the defenses of Boich in the fields facing the river. If we had attacked in the direction the Germans had expected, we would have had much more difficulty.

The battalion aid station is in the living room of a German house in a small village nestled behind a ridge overlooking the Roer. The medical officer has no patients to care for, as all of the wounded have already been evacuated back across the Roer. He tells me to lean over a table and rapidly cuts away the old dressing. Yesterday was a busy day for him, he tells me, and then he paints my wound, assures me that it will heal in a few days, and puts a new dressing on it. He then gives me a tetanus shot and fills out a casualty tag.

"Well, you've now got a Purple Heart, Lieutenant!"

"One is enough, thanks."

The jeep ride back to Boich is uneventful, and I notice that our mortars have been moved forward into Boich. They are emplaced in a field between two buildings. I find Lieutenant Ciccone, who is relieved to hear that my wound is so slight. He tells me that he heard only that I was wounded and was "sweating me out." We now address ourselves to the problem of finding me a new pair of pants. After numerous inquiries, we find a soldier with an extra pair of trousers, just barely large enough for me to wear. I am happy to shed the ripped pair, since about half of my leg is exposed to the cold while wearing it.

The next day it occurs to me that I had better write home before the message about me being wounded in action arrives:

> I just happened to remember that when you get medical treatment for a wound, however slight, there is a report sent home saying only that I have been wounded. I have heard so many tales of families who have been needlessly worried by these reports, that I hasten to write you, in case you get one of these reports.
>
> The story is simple. Two days ago I got a slight hit on the right leg from a fragment. It was so minor that I didn't go to the aid station until the next day, as we were too busy. . . . My leg was stiff for a while, mostly gone now. So please remember, I don't lie—so don't worry! . . . Don't forget, I'm okay, and still pitching, We've got 'em on the run, and to do that we have to do a lot of running too. . . . We are hoping for big things here, and I hope we aren't disappointed. I don't think we will be.

The following day, the first of March, L Company marches out of Boich and takes up the movement to the east. We pass through village after village. In some there are signs of bitter fighting; in others we can see that only a half-hearted resistance has been made. Soller, Stockheim, and Jakobwuellesheim are now behind us, and we halt in the town of Kelz for the night.

Being still in the battalion reserve, we have much time to ourselves, and along with many others, I address myself to the job of writing home:

Marched far today, so you see my leg is all right, and anybody who can keep up with the American Infantry has to be in top shape.

I wish to heaven I could tell you what we're doing, where we are, and how things are going; for my soul is bubbling with joy. Why? Because this is Germany that is getting blasted. Those refugees are Germans—those houses in ruins are German—those prisoners you see are German. Yes, if anything gives satisfaction, it is a little retaliation for the beating that Dad saw the English and the French take. This is the payment for the destroyed Liege, Rotterdam, London; and all the rest . . .

. . . We have been fortunate in having wonderful weather for fighting, brisk and little rain. . . .

. . . I hope some day to be able to explain my philosophy to you. You would see then that there is no reason to worry. For every discomfort we have, Jerry undergoes three times as much. Then too, we are not always uncomfortable. I have been in countless cellars, houses, and even dugouts that had all of the comforts of home.

I believe that I forgot to tell you people that I have purchased another watch. The one Dad gave me was perfect except that you couldn't read it at night. Phosphorus too dull. So about a month ago I got hold of a PX officer who was selling watches to officers and got one for 900 Belgian fr. or 1100 fr. French, or about $22.00 good old American simoleons. It is very phosphorescent; in fact, so bright that I have to black it out at night. Runs well. I gave my other watch to a Sgt. who needed one. I loaned it, and he will return it when he gets the new one he's looking for.

Lost a lot of good friends lately, and hope they won't be back before the war ends. I hope, in other words, that this will be over soon.

Don't let the people go to sleep, tho, as there is *beaucoup* war left.

The next day we move forward again, marching to Gladbach. After dark we march to the town of Erp. As we enter the town, I see one of our jeeps burning brightly by the side of the road. We pass through this town, with orders to attack it. As our troops are held up at the entrance to the large town of Lechenich, our long column moves down the darkened road. Now a German aircraft flies down the road toward us, dropping small antipersonnel bombs on our highway. None of them strike near me, and I hear no news of casualties from this attack. We can hear the roar of small-arms fire as we approach the town of Lechenich from the southwest. A railroad line runs along our highway on the right edge of the road. We pass an occasional blackened German truck or armored vehicle.

Now we are at the edge of the town. We can barely make out the mass of houses against the dark sky. There is a burst of firing to our left front. Next the column moves across a railroad yard. Sniper fire whips overhead every few minutes, and we crouch behind railroad cars, then move forward again. We find ourselves moving through another company, and these soldiers tell us in no uncertain terms of the tough time they had trying to take the town. Our column moves on. All is quiet ahead now.

Word passes back along the line to move into the large houses in the town and await further orders. Potts and I move into a large cellar with a squad of riflemen. Soon the lads are busy opening trunks and suitcases, rifling through stored clothing, and searching shelves for food or liquor. A soldier holds up a large Nazi flag he has found in a trunk. "Does anybody want this?" I think it makes a fine souvenir and take it. I fold it neatly and stick it in a pocket of my field jacket. I notice a swastika armband on the floor and stick this too in my pocket. We discover nothing else of interest in the cellar, and soon the order comes to move on.

We move as silently as possible down the dark streets leading into the center of town, hugging the walls of the houses, ready to dart into doorways at any suspicious sound. Progress is slow as the leading squads must enter and search each house for Germans. The night wears on, and we move a bit and halt, move a bit and halt. We cross a stream running through the town. I see the huge shape of a tank standing in the darkened main street near the bridge; no one pays any attention to it.

We proceed down the main street. A few minutes later, we hear behind us the sound of a motor starting, then the unmistakable sound of a tank moving. The sound of the tank dies away far to the rear. A few minutes later the grapevine passes forward the word that the tank we passed was German, that the crew was asleep inside, and that when they discovered that Americans were all around them, they simply drove out of town. No one had a weapon available to stop them. "Jesus H. Christ!" A soldier speaks from behind me in the dark. "I had my shoulder up against that tank when we halted back there. I thought it was one of ours!"

Now L Company has reached the far edge of Lechenich, and reports come back that the Germans have evacuated the town. I move forward with Potts to find Captain Ritter, who is busy organizing a platoon-sized patrol to move on down the main highway out of town to the east. "About a mile and a half down, there is the Erft Canal," he says. "Division wants the bridge over it seized. Price, go along with the platoon and give them any mortar fire they need. I'm sending along the heavy machine guns with them."

"Yes, sir, Captain." At about three o'clock in the morning

we start our march out of town. I walk just behind the two leading squads with the platoon leader. We are on a raised highway
that runs almost due east from Lechenich. The men march in
single file, one file on each shoulder of the road. We are intensely
tired, and the stillness of the night adds to the eerie atmosphere. Finally we arrive at the canal. The faint glow in the sky
in the east gives us just enough light to see across the canal. The
column halts and the word is passed back in whispers: "The
bridge is already blown."

Suddenly, every man in front of me dives silently over the
side of the raised highway on which we are standing. Potts and
I follow suit, diving to the ground on the right side of the road.
From my position on the ground, I can see that there is a German vehicle on the road just across the canal, and a group of
German soldiers are throwing themselves to the sides of their
road. Not a shot is fired. The distance between the Germans
and our leading riflemen is only about thirty yards. Neither side
wants to open fire from the raised roadways.

I have a different idea, however, and soon have the headset
of the radio in my hand, trying to call back to the mortar platoon. I want to bring fire on the Germans, but I get no answer
from the mortars. I can see our platoon leader splitting his force,
sending half to dig in on the left of the highway and half on my
side of the highway. In a few minutes it is light enough to see
across the blown bridge clearly, and we realize the Germans have
disappeared. They probably crawled backward until they were
able to withdraw in safety.

With the coming of dawn, the first round of German mortar fire arrives. They know our position accurately, and soon our
area is being subjected to an intense barrage. This is heavy stuff.
Probably 160-mm mortars. They cause tremendous explosions
when the shells land. Potts and I find ourselves digging for all

we are worth into the road embankment. The ground is some-what rocky, but not as bad as it could be. From time to time I stop digging to try the radio again, but there is no answer from the other end. The platoon leader sends word that he has notified the company commander that the bridge is blown. His orders are to dig in and hold the bridge site.

Now it begins to snow. The temperature has dropped rap-idly, and the light coating of snowflakes changes the appear-ance of the landscape. When I have dug a hole large enough to hold all of my body, except my head and arms, I crawl in and begin to wait out the mortar fire. At that moment, from some-where across the Erft Canal, a German tank opens fire. His tar-get is on the long, raised highway behind us. I crawl up to the roadway and look to the rear. Far down the highway, I can see a truck turning around and speeding back into Lechenich. The German tank has us cut off from all support in that direction.

The tank stops firing, and the mortar fire ceases. Inexplica-bly, our radio begins to operate properly and I am able to call for a fire mission from the mortars. I decide to plaster the road and trees just across the canal just in case there is a German defensive position there. I call for area fire and soon have our rounds falling on the other side of the canal. This does not seem to stop the German mortar fire, and we are subjected to a few rounds every once in a while throughout the morning.

The word comes back to me that one of the German mor-tar rounds has killed Sergeant Manelli, a machine gunner of M Company and one of Father Bracken's best friends. I find myself wondering how Bracken is doing. He is at his post with the machine guns just about fifty yards in front of me on the edge of the canal. They are dug into some bushes that line the water's edge. I begin to call for mortar fire on more distant tar-gets. A house standing near the highway to our left is my next target, then I drop shells just over a ridge in the direction of a large factory to our left front. The tops of the factory chimneys are just visible over the ridge.

Finally, the enemy fire stops, and I call a halt to my own firing. Shortly afterward, a foot messenger, obviously very tired, arrives from Lechenich. He squats down by my foxhole and asks me where Father is, adding, "They want him back at the CP. Rotation, I guess." I point out his position ahead of me. "No kidding! Boy, that's great!" The messenger moves down to the bushes to deliver his news. A few minutes later I see Father emerge from the bushes. He stops to talk with man after man dug in along the road embankment. Then he sees me and walks over to my hole. His face bears an unforgettable look of astonishment and mock curiosity.

"Lieutenant! Did you hear? They want me back at the CP! Now, what do you suppose they want? I just can't figure it out. What do you suppose they want, Lieutenant?"

"Well, Father, why don't you go back and find out."

Bracken thinks about this for a while. I can imagine what he is feeling. After so many years of war, he is afraid to believe that he might be rotated to the States for fear that it might turn out to be a mistake. Finally, he nods his head vigorously and says, "Yes, sir, Lieutenant, I'd better just go back and find out." He rises to his feet and begins to walk back toward safety. "Good luck, Father," I call to him. He waves his hand over his head, and I watch him walk out of sight. It looks like he is going to make it.

Just as it is growing dark, I make out a column of our troops moving toward the canal about a mile to our right. They receive a tremendous barrage of artillery fire, each explosion making a bright orange-colored flash in the night. I can see through my field glasses that they do not halt but continue to move across the canal. I wonder if they have a bridge or are wading across a shallow point. Possibly, they are swimming across. There is the continual sound of artillery and small-arms fire on our right during most of the night, and due to this activity, few of us get any sleep.

With the coming of dawn the next day, the front is quiet, and I spend much of my time up on the road observing to the front. A truck comes safely to us during the morning and unloads rations. I notice a good deal of excitement around the spot where the rations are being issued and walk over and find that a new and ingenious type of ration has appeared: cans of celery soup. A black-powder fuse projects from the top of each can. Inside the can, this fuse is enclosed in a metal cylinder running from the top to the bottom of the can. I discover that you simply light the fuse at the top, and the fuse inside the can burns slowly down to the bottom of the can, heating the contents.

I am delighted with the invention. Celery soup is one of my favorites, and *hot* celery soup borders on the luxurious. Several of the soldiers give me their cans. They simply do not like celery soup. Their loss is my gain. I pull my spoon from its constant storage place—the right breast pocket of my field jacket—and am soon in hog heaven. I watch as one soldier lights the fuse to his can and throws it at another soldier. He yells, "Grenade!" The hissing sound of the burning fuse is quite realistic.

At night, a group of combat engineers throws a complete treadway bridge over the canal at the point where the old bridge stood. I am amazed to see the speed and efficiency with which they work. As soon as they are finished, they lose no time in mounting their vehicles and disappearing down the road to the rear. I sleep in my foxhole covered with a blanket. It is the first sleep I have had in several days.

The next day, the fourth, we are finally ordered to rejoin L Company in Lechenich, and we march back up the long highway to the town. The rest of the company has been resting for two days, and there is a lot of kidding going on between the "rear echelon" and the "Erft Canal" groups. I borrow a V-mail blank and write another short letter home. I tell them about the two swastikas I have mailed home, then add, "I have been doing much lately, and we are doing wonderful jobs as ever, this is the best division in the army. I am in perfect health, and last night I slept all night—first sleep in two days. Once again we wait for a while. Very fast moving outfit . . . . Here it is March already— my how time flies. Each day, though, seems like a century. My feet are holding up fine. Hope yours are the same. . . . Keep your fingers crossed for an early peace."

A soldier sticks his head through the door. "Lieutenant, do you like canned cherries? We found a whole lot in a cellar."

"Thank you very much!" Out comes the spoon from the pocket, and I slowly make my way through a quart jar of delicious cherries. They are just a little bitter tasting, but make a very fine meal. I find out that L Company has a new commander, Captain Schuler. I feel almost like I have lost my older brother in hearing of Captain Ritter's leaving the unit, but I am happy that he is now out of danger.

Two days later we receive orders to swing to the south and seize two towns lying only a few miles from the Rhine River. Our objective is about half way between the large German cities of Cologne and Bonn. We move by motor part of the distance, and then, just at dusk, begin our march through a dense forest. Inside the forest the darkness is intense.

Our planned route should bring us out of the forest just at the edge of the town of Walbeberg, which is our first objective. The forest is about three miles wide, and after we have been marching for about a mile, the whispered command, "Down!" is passed back along the lines. We all hit the ground, and then there is a deathly silence. I wonder why we have stopped, and after about ten minutes on the ground, the column arises again, and resumes the march. We cross a main highway that runs north and south through the forest. At the edge of the highway, a sergeant tells me that the leading squad heard a large German foot column moving along the highway and, tactfully, hit the dirt and allowed the column to pass across our front. The reasoning seemed to be that Jerry was headed directly into our lines to the south and a firefight with them could have given away our surprise attack to the east.

Now the column crosses the highway, and once again we are in the dense forest. We move, then halt, then move again, following small trails that at times seem to disappear. To our front we can hear the sound of small-arms fire and artillery shells exploding. The column seems to guide itself on the firing, and finally our files emerge from the forest. Directly to our right front we hear the sounds of firing within a small town. I move forward, and a platoon leader tells me that we have come out of the forest far to the south of where we should be. We will turn north and move up to the towns we are to seize.

Now that we are out of the forest, we find that there is considerable visibility from the moonlight. We skirt the edge of the forest as we move to the north. After about half an hour's march, the head of our column reaches the outskirts of Walbeberg. The leading platoon begins its house-to-house search. Soon reports are flowing back that the houses are deserted but show every evidence of being lived in. A few German soldiers, deserters, are found hiding in some of the houses. I move ahead with the company commander, who wants to secure his objective before daylight.

The town of Schwadorf adjoins Walbeberg, with a railroad line acting as the boundary between the two towns. Soon we are at the edge of Walbeberg, and we turn east toward the Rhine River and our next objective. We are on a main business street, and in the moonlight the heavily shuttered business establishments look extremely foreboding. In an instant, the stillness is shattered by an artillery round that comes at our small party from the east straight up the street. It explodes against a store front with terrific force, and the flash of the explosion lights up the street. We hit the hard pavement in all directions; there is no cover. Splinters from the shell fill the air, ricocheting in crazy patterns off the hard street and building surfaces. Someone has spotted or heard our movement.

We hug the curbs and doorways, and another shell explodes in approximately the same position. I hear a flurry of excited talk from a group of men. After a long period of time, the shelling stops, and I walk over to the company commander. Captain Schuler tells me that a shell fragment went through his canteen, and that when he felt the liquid running down his leg, he thought he had been hit. He makes quite a joke out of it, and asks me if "being shot through the canteen" will bring him a Purple Heart.

Schuler quickly sends his leading platoon down side streets, avoiding the main street, which is now under enemy fire. It is not long before a messenger brings the news that they have found a bunker completely full of German civilians who have taken shelter from our night attack. The captain and I proceed to the air-raid shelter, and I spend a few minutes talking to a representative of the town's people. He states that the people have been in the bunker for days, not knowing when their town would be attacked. The German civilian tells me that the civilians refuse to be evacuated across the Rhine and want to live in their homes. We continue to search the town of Schwadorf, and finally we clear the town to its eastern edge. I look at my map and see that we are now only three miles from the Rhine. It is the morning of the seventh of March. In only ten days we have come from the Roer to the Rhine.

After spending a sleepless night, during which we prepared for a possible counterattack from the east, I receive orders the next morning to remain in one of the towns we have captured as an acting military government officer until further notice. On this day the German civilians return to their homes. These people are Rhinelanders and proud of their differences with the rest of Germany. My first order is to establish a strict curfew on any movement after dark. A few minutes after I have spread this word, I am visited by a German nurse, Frau Ingels, who states that there are two women in the town who are expecting children this very night. Could I give her permission to travel on the streets during the night in case she is needed as the midwife? I give her a pass.

I meet Pastor Fassbender and the town policeman, Herr Gessner, and ask their help in the wording of a proclamation that we will publish at the church directing people to the acting mayor in the event that they have problems. I appoint a Herr Baum as mayor upon the recommendation of the pastor and some other seemingly responsible persons. In the afternoon I have the adult population collected in the large church of the town and stand by the altar as the pastor instructs the people on the curfew and the other details of the occupation. I watch the reaction as he tells the civilians that all firearms, including shotguns, must be turned in to the military government. The crowd is passive and seems to accept the various rules without question.

I have billeted myself with a German family. There is a young boy in the family, a handsome lad of about ten, who is completely indoctrinated into an adoration for Hitler and the

German Army. In the evening, his mother asks me what I think of the German soldiers. I reply truthfully that they are outstanding soldiers in almost all respects. Out of the corner of my eye I see the young boy swell with pride. In order to deflate him a bit, I add that Germany is defeated and must bear the consequences of starting the war. The lad can not bear to hear this and jumps to his feet. "The war is not lost! Our secret weapons will destroy you!"

His blind, fanatical attitude makes me lose my temper. I can not help but remember the good comrades who have fallen while fighting against just such fanaticism. I order the boy to leave the room and tell his mother that she should tell her son the facts of life concerning the so-called secret weapons—weapons that simply do not exist. A few minutes later I am ashamed at losing my temper with a small boy. I put it down to the emotional strain of being an infantryman, then forget the whole thing.

I am besieged with callers during my short stay as military governor. The electricity does not work, and someone will have to go to the large town of Brühl, a mile to the north, to notify the electric company. Several others report German deserters are hiding in their house. A mother pleads with me that her seventeen-year-old soldier son is hiding at home. She does not want him to be taken as a prisoner of war. I try to assure her that he will be released soon, but that if he was a soldier, he must surrender himself. She leaves in tears.

On the seventh I write home again. My first thought is about my brother, Hickham, who I believed to be on his way from the South Pacific to the States:

> Once again I am in a hurry, but I must write to tell you I am constantly thinking of you. I hope Hick is on his way home, and that you will remember to give him all of the affection

that is possible. All soldiers crave affection, but shy from it at first; but give them a little time, then lay it on.

The German civilians the towns are full of are a queer lot. We are suspicious of all of them. They fear the Russians worse than sin, and are pretty happy that we are Americans. . . . I wish I could get your mail one at a time, but in the Infantry it is usually a bunch every week.

Four days later I am ordered to rejoin M Company in the town of Sechtem. Here I am instructed that I will proceed to the bank of the Rhine and observe across the river for possible German movements. Potts and I set out in a jeep and drive to the remains of a huge artificial gasoline plant near the town of Widdig. A platoon of infantrymen are billeted in houses just behind the plant. They tell me that all is quiet across the Rhine, and that they have a lookout posted near the top of the main plant building. The building itself is eight stories high, and I decide that the top will make an outstanding observation post.

I pass through the ground floor of the plant and am amazed at the destruction caused by the aerial bombardment of the plant. The soldiers tell me that this bombing took place at night, and yet, as far as I can tell, not a bomb fell outside of the plant grounds. Huge pieces of machinery litter the lower floors, and gaping holes appear in floors and ceilings. Potts and I climb metal stairs, up and up until finally we are at the top. I move forward and see two of our riflemen gazing out across the Rhine River, which flows close to the foot of the plant. All the window glass has been shattered, and I find a spot from which I can observe for miles to the east across the river.

Radio communications are excellent from this observation post, and I bring fire on two targets during the two days I am at the plant. On one occasion I see a squad of German soldiers crawling behind some railroad cars about seven hundred yards across the river. I fire about fifty rounds of high explosive at them and have the satisfaction of seeing them disappear on the run down the railroad tracks leading to the south. I do not know if I scored any hits. On another occasion I see some German soldiers climbing aboard one of the long river barges moored against the other side of the Rhine. I call for fire but find it extremely difficult to hit the target. My white phosphorus rounds make a beautiful white cloud when they strike the surface of the river. Finally, I switch to high explosive, and I am rewarded by seeing one of my shells land on the deck of the barge. I throw a few more at the barge but see no further movement on it during the rest of the day.

After arriving at the plant the next day, I alternate between scanning the terrain through my field glasses and writing a letter to my parents. I describe the accurate bombing of the plant to them, and then my thoughts turn to the future. We all realize that the war against Japan will not be over for a long time. We have the Pacific theater staring us in the face:

> And so the days pass by, and we wonder many things. All of us have had our hopes blasted so much that we no longer speak of Germany surrendering. We fear that they will fight on and on. But cheering news on all fronts makes us all feel good, and we read that we can expect about three weeks at home before going to the Pacific. God grant that the war will also be over before that comes about.
>
> Yes, the days pass, and I pull and twist the ends of my mustache, and chew gum to keep my teeth cleansed, and write to have others write me. We live a neat, orderly simple life. All of our belongings must be carried, so they are few. I shed my knit sleeveless sweater the other day. The one you sent me at Camp Stewart, remember? It was worn ever since I left the States.

Now all I wear is field jacket, shirt OD, long-sleeved wool knit sweater, and long underwear, in order from outside.

The *Stars and Stripes* brings us the wonderful news that a bridge has been seized across the Rhine at Remagen, to the south of us. All of us resign ourselves to the fact that if there is heavy fighting to be done, we will be sent to do it. And just as we predicted, on the fourteenth of March I am called back to the heavy-weapons company command post to receive the order that will send us into the Remagen bridgehead the next day.

Captain Nechey and his executive officer, Lieutenant Volk, brief the observers and platoon leaders on the movement. I jot down key phrases in my notebook as they speak. Through the windows of the room we can see the ceaseless movement of our military vehicles and an occasional passing German civilian. "We move out at 8 in the morning. . . . Vehicles can't recross the bridge once they are over. . . . One day full rations, and squad rolls. . . . As much ammunition as we can carry. . . . All jeeps to carry ammunition signs. . . . Use Halazone tablets in all drinking water. . . . Everything must be camouflaged . . ." The voices drone on. We become more alert as the opposition is mentioned: "277th Volkgrenadiers, 11th Panzer Division, 106th Panzer Division." We are warned that there will be both German and Allied planes overhead. Antiaircraft machine guns are to be mounted, and air guards will be stationed on each vehicle.

The schedule of colored panels to be displayed on our vehicles is the next order of business. We use them so that our aircraft can identify us: "14 to 19 March, red and yellow panels; 20 to 25 March, single red panel; 26 to 31 March, single yellow panel. Order of march: Headquarters Company, I, K, L, and M Companies." Now the route of march to the bridgehead is given to us: "Weilerswist, Metternich, Heimerzheim, Morenhoven, Stadt

Meckenheim, Gelsdorf, and then east to Kripp." I look at my map and see that our route parallels the Rhine and stays about eight miles to the west of the river for most of the way. Nestor, Hubbard, and I get busy copying the dozens of artillery concentration map coordinates that we will use inside the bridgehead.

That afternoon I write another one of my before-action letters to my mother. As usual, I do not wish to alarm her in any way, and to mention an impending move would be a terrific breach of security:

14 MARCH 1945
GERMANY

DEAREST MOTHER,

I believe I have been making a great mistake for a long time that you don't know about. I never, or at least rarely, mention letters I receive from you. And so you don't think your letters are arriving. But they are, and I am happy. For instance yesterday a V (25 Feb), today 2 Vs (26 and 28 Feb). So you see they are coming right along. . . .

Mother, I appreciate your thoughts and prayers, and I can feel you rooting for me all the time. Keep it up, and don't let anything get you down. And don't lavish too much attention on me; remember that you have two other men who love you very dearly, and they need you as much, or more, than I do. . . .

You asked me to ask prisoners why Germany goes on fighting. They say, "We can't quit. *Die Regierung!* (The rulers), the Gestapo, and Hitler won't let us," or, "Unconditional surrender will make slaves of us. We will be taken from our homes," or, "We fear the Russians, and must fight on against them, and since you are their allies, we must fight you also."

On the next day, just before we move out, I carefully draw a picture of my mustache, which is now about three inches from tip to tip, and enclose it with the letter.

It is the fifteenth of March. Skillfully, and with a minimum of confusion, the jeeps, three-quarter-ton trucks, and two-and-a-half ton trucks of M Company move out at the rear of the 3d Battalion column. I sit in the front seat with another soldier and the driver of the jeep. In the rear seat, three more soldiers are seated on piles of equipment. In the trailer we are towing are scores of rounds of mortar ammunition. Seated on the ammunition, their legs dangling over the trailer sides, are five more soldiers. The jeep motor roars steadily and seems to make no objection to the heavy load.

7

REMAGEN BRIDGEHEAD

The entire battalion is motorized for the trip to Remagen. Early in the morning we swing back to the west to avoid enemy observation from across the Rhine, then head south to our destination. Mere words can not describe the organized confusion that reigns as we draw near to the bridge itself. At times we wait in columns for hours without moving, at other times the road contains two and even three columns of jeeps and trucks, all rolling parallel to each other and all heading for the bridge. As we draw closer to the bridge, we see antiaircraft machine guns and guns everywhere.

German artillery fire drops about the bridge in the fields beside us. We quickly push wrecked and burning trucks from the roads, and from time to time every antiaircraft weapon within miles opens up with a deafening roar at some real or imaginary German aircraft flying above. I feel sorry for our own fighter pilots assigned to air-cover duty over the bridgehead. Due to the necessity of protecting the bridge, the ack-ack boys are firing first and looking later. At any rate, they do their job well, as many days later the bridge, weakened by aerial bombing and artillery fire, finally collapses into the Rhine. Yet I feel helpless, sitting in my stationary jeep, hemmed in on all sides by other jeeps and trucks, expecting at each moment that one of the artillery shells will fall in my lap.

Slowly but surely we draw ahead and finally see that we are to cross the Rhine on a pontoon bridge about four hundred yards south of the captured railway bridge. An artificial fog hangs over the river from our chemical smoke generators; they serve their purpose well by not permitting the Germans any direct observation of the bridges. As we cross the long pontoon bridge I can make out the tanks and trucks crossing the railway bridge in a steady stream. The entire picture is very heartening, since infantrymen rarely have a chance to see so much of their own army at a glance. The sight of massed men and materiel gives me a feeling of invincibility that lasts for a long time.

On the other side of the Rhine we drive through a railway underpass, turn left into Erpel, and then east up a dirt road leading into the hills. Once out of the village the terrain becomes rugged and lonely, and for the next week we catch only occasional glimpses of towns or villages. Almost at dark we go into bivouac in a gully at the edge of a forest. The first thing I see as we enter the forest is a torn and bloody American gas mask lying on the ground. As we are well within range of the German artillery, we immediately dig in, felling trees to use as top cover. Once our holes are sufficiently deep, we post our sentries and fall into a sound sleep.

On the following day, the sixteenth of March, we move out by motor for a few miles, then dismount and continue by foot. Before long, German artillery shells begin to drop around our column, but the forest gives us shelter from observation and the shelling damages only our nerves. As we move along the forest trails, we pass three of our Sherman tanks, which were destroyed by German tank fire on the previous day. The holes in their turrets make it look as though the metal tanks are made of butter, so little resistance they offered to the projectiles. We proceed up a steep, wooded slope and take up a position on top of a hill for the night. The ground here is shale and rock, so no digging is possible. We build small walls out of the rocks for protection against shell fragments, and I stretch my rubber poncho over the rocks as a roof. It does little good, as rain during the night pours through the neck hole of the poncho.

The next day, the seventeenth, we move out after a cold breakfast of K rations and take up our march again. Around noon we come under heavy German artillery fire while halted waiting for orders. The dirt flies as we dig slit trenches. It is a very disagreeable hour for us, as we have to remain in our position and can do nothing about the shells, which are crashing into the tree tops and trucks and raining fragments down onto the ground. Soon the fire becomes infrequent, and our wonderful kitchen personnel serves up a hot lunch for us while we wait to move on. Later in the afternoon we again begin to march. During this phase of the attack, it should be noted, our battalion is in reserve and our marching is without any contact with the enemy. When we halt in the evening, we find that L company, to which I am as usual attached, will lead off in a night attack. Our objective: the Frankfurt-Cologne autobahn. And an important objective it is. The giant four-lane highway has been a great German asset during the Remagen fighting, and possession of it has enabled the Germans to switch their troops and artillery rapidly to the north or south of the bridgehead.

Elaborate precautions are taken to make the attack succeed.

From back near the Rhine, searchlight units aim their brilliant beams on the clouds overhead, giving us an unnatural but highly effective moonlight. But even this illumination does not penetrate the darkness of the forest through which our route of approach leads. Therefore, parties of engineers stretch hundreds of yards of mine tape (a white cloth tape usually used for marking cleared portions of minefields) from tree to tree, marking a path for the advancing riflemen. Despite this, we march for hours in almost utter darkness. In many places it is necessary to hold onto the entrenching tool dangling from the belt of the man ahead in order to keep direction. It is astonishing how quietly and smoothly we file through the forest. Suddenly, the trees end, and the autobahn lies only a few paces ahead. From the right front the stillness is broken by the sound of a machine gun firing long bursts. An occasional rifle shot adds to the din. Then silence. The column, which hit the dirt with alacrity, gets to its feet and moves on. After climbing a short slope I find myself on the autobahn, and in the dim artificial light I can make out the bodies of several men lying on and just off the far side of the highway. An unknown soldier standing on the autobahn whispers to me, "We caught a whole platoon of them marching along the autobahn. They never knew what hit them!"

We move across the autobahn and proceed up a small trail, constantly climbing. After a twenty-minute march we are at the edge of an extremely deep quarry, which fortunately has a road-like ledge running around most of its circumference. L Company moves to the right and around the edge of the quarry. Before we are able take up our positions to the right and forward of the quarry, Jerry becomes active. With typical speed, salvo after salvo of German artillery falls into our position, as the Germans, realizing the blunder they committed in not defending the quarry, attempt to shell us out of the position. The next morning, the eighteenth, it becomes apparent that we are holding the highest piece of ground for miles, and the importance of the position becomes clearer.

And so the digging begins. It takes only a few minutes to discover that the ground around the stone quarry is, as expected, rocky. Digging is extremely difficult. I dig into a bank about five yards from the company commander's position, and by daylight I have scooped out a hole in the side of the bank that is about two feet deep at the bottom. By lying on my back, with my head and shoulders bending sharply upward and my feet above my head, knees almost touching my helmet, I am able to place approximately half of my body in this hole. As absurd as it sounds, I sleep several nights in this position—if you can call it sleep.

With the coming of dawn, after a sleepless night, my work as an observer begins in earnest. Taking Potts with me, I look for observation posts. I can hear occasional rounds of small-arms fire, and intermittent artillery fire continues to fall around the almost circular quarry. (You can get some idea of the size of the quarry when you consider that three rifle companies are stretched out around the lip of the depression.) In walking about the rim of the quarry, I notice many of the outlying riflemen have constructed shelters from the abundant stone, finding digging in the stone ground to be too difficult a task.

As I search for observation posts, I realize that no one position gives me a commanding view, and that necessitates moving from point to point and registering mortar fire from many observation posts. One day, after clambering over the high bank that separates the road around the inside quarry edge from the surrounding ground, a German sniper hidden in the dense underbrush that covers the entire area fires a single round at us. The bullet passes between Potts and myself. Since both of us are armed only with pistols, we scramble down the bank again, catch our breath, and then decide to move about one hundred yards along the quarry edge before attempting to go over the bank again. Due to the denseness of the underbrush, we see neither hide nor hair of the German when we climb up over the bank at the new spot.

Later, Potts and I are out on an exposed slope in front of the quarry, standing about thirty feet apart, when we hear, softly at first, then growing ever louder, the roar of an incoming shell. From the sound of the shell I immediately can tell two things: this is the largest caliber shell I have ever heard, and the shell is aimed for the exact spot on which I stand. Being a large shell, it moves extremely slowly through the air, and it seems to take minutes before it hits the ground. I run, knowing that I have to put a lot of space between myself and the explosion. The second before the shell hits, I throw myself to the ground, feet toward the shell. The earth heaves, and my ears are deafened by the roar of the explosion. The blast of air tears my helmet from my head and sends it rolling twenty yards away. As suddenly as it has exploded, there comes a deathly quiet, punctuated only by the throbbing ringing in my ears. Then I hear the frantic voice of Potts. "Lieutenant! Lieutenant!"

I sit up and see that at the sound of the shell, Potts ran in the opposite direction. The hole the shell has dug in the ground is exactly where I was standing when I first heard it. I get to my feet, and Potts, on joining me, says he thought the shell "had hit me for sure." We decide we do not like this area and proceed just over the ledge to the quarry road again. And who should we meet as we clamber down the slope but our M Company commander, Nechey, who sarcastically asks us why the hell we are not observing. I am on the point of blurting out the story of the shell when I realize that this will make no impression whatsoever, and so, without a word, we climb back up the bank and find a new observation post.

The tremendous shelling of our position reminds me that it might not be a bad idea to write another letter to my parents. I borrow a V-mail, and scrawl a message, which, for all I know, may be my last. I date it the nineteenth of March: "Once again I am forced to use V-mail, being so damn far from stationery that it isn't funny. We have been having a rough old time, but we're doing good work. We all wonder when Jerry will capitulate, but he is a stubborn bastard." I tell them how glad I am to hear that my brother has been promoted to captain: "I wish I could have a picture of my view from my observation post. Miles of rolling Germany. With artillery breaking all over it, and planes strafing, bombing, and dropping incendiaries. The sun is out and despite a night in a muddy hole in a bank, and the fact that rheumatic pains have got me, I'm pretty comfortable, seeing the sun is toasting the back of my neck. I miss you people, oh so much, and am looking forward to that big reunion supper when we can really talk this thing over. And now until next time, I love you very much."

On one occasion we watch as another division on the right of the 1st Division makes an attack on a German-held village just to the south of the quarry. As in so many other actions, the 1st Division has pushed out far beyond the divisions on the flanks, and the attack is an attempt by the other division to come on line with the 1st. The attack is made by about two companies with a few tanks, in the rear firing over the heads of the infantrymen. Unfortunately, the riflemen have to advance over very level and open ground, and well-aimed German artillery fire, coupled with mortar and machine-gun fire, soon have the advancing line punched full of holes, stopped, wavering, and then withdrawing. The entire action takes only a few minutes, and before long I have my mortars dropping round after round into the places where I imagine the German defenders to be. To the credit of the division attacking, barely fifteen minutes pass before they launch their attack again, and with the help of some American artillery fire, the concentrated tank fire, and, I hope, my mortar fire, they soon advance into the village, which is just out of sight from my position. All that afternoon we hear the bursts of machine gun and small-arms fire coming from the vicinity of the village, and then all falls quiet again. Our flank is protected!

On another occasion, during a comparatively quiet period, a single shot is fired from one of our infantry outposts, dug in among the rocks on an exposed slope. Soon the cry "Medic!" is relayed along the line. And then, a few minutes later, "Stretcher bearer!" is passed from hole to hole. A few minutes pass again, and then two tired, dirty medics come through the gully past the company command post carrying the stretcher, on which lies one of our soldiers. He grimaces and moans in pain, and his face is white. But despite his pain, he casts embarrassed and fearful looks at his company commander as he passes. The first medic mutters, "Self-inflicted" as they pass the commander. No one speaks or moves until the stretcher is out of sight, and no one speaks of the incident or the soldier again.

After days of continual shelling, our minds seem to black out at times. Our casualties are not heavy, but they are constant. There is no hole deep enough to escape from the fragments and the air bursts; there is no chance to wash or dry damp clothing;

and, more important, there is no chance to get away from the shells. Finally, however, it ends. Our Air Force, we discover, was active all along the front, strafing gun positions, machine-gunning troops and convoys. And then, as usual, we receive orders to advance again.

Our new objective is a German fighter airfield lying about three miles farther to the east. We have heard rumors of the existence of this airfield throughout our stay at the quarry, but since we have not been able to locate it on any of the maps available, we have passed it off as an idle rumor. In reality, the airfield is very rough and temporary. The Germans merely cleared the trees from a portion of the forest between Wuellscheid and Germscheid, leveled it a bit, and that was it. Two fairly large buildings for offices and quarters located on the south edge of the field complete the picture.

Our advance from the quarry begins late in the afternoon of the nineteenth. Filing from the quarry, we march along the sides of the road to Stockhausen, which was captured the previous day by other units. While en route our column is strafed by one of our fighter planes, resulting in only minor damage to one of our vehicles. We soundly curse the Air Force, but actually, there is little to distinguish us from the retreating German columns a few hundred yards to our front. At Stockhausen, the road turns slightly to the north and we begin our advance to the airfield. Darkness has fallen, but the night is quite bright—too bright for comfort. We advance as silently as possible, casting glances into the forests that line both sides of the road. As usual, in our imaginations we see the most fantastic things. At one point I swear I see a column of men moving parallel to our column about fifty yards to our left. But the appearance of our flank guards a few seconds later proves the impossibility of this vision. The stillness of the night is broken only by the crunch of our footsteps and the occasional rumble of artillery shells falling on the airfield to our front.

As the head of our column comes to the edge of the airfield, German artillery, with their usual accuracy, begins dropping shells on our column. On reaching the field, L Company leading, we turn left to seize the two airfield buildings. The remainder of the battalion turns right and follows the road to the end of the airfield, the limit of the battalion attack. As we clear the buildings of the few remaining Germans, most of them sick and wounded, we hear intense small-arms fire and artillery in the direction the other companies of our battalion have taken. We have been lucky again! The Germans fight bitterly to hold the high ground at the eastern edge of the airfield.

All is not completely serene at the airfield buildings, however. During the night, German artillery falls intermittently on and around the buildings in which L Company is located. I select as my observation post the top of some cellar stairs, which lead into the basement of the administration building. Almost immediately upon beginning my observation across the airfield I make out what appears to be a long column of troops marching single file across the airfield, their heads and shoulders visible, the rest of their bodies below the skyline. I send my runner to report this to the company commander and call over my radio for registration fire on the column. The L Company commander soon joins me but is unable to discern the moving column in the darkness. After wasting precious moments convincing him that the column is there, I am asked over the radio if the column I have sighted might be friendly troops. I answer with some impatience that it is headquarters' job to tell me, and that as far as I am concerned, they are Jerries. A few more precious minutes slip by before permission is granted for me to open fire. By this time, the column is completely out of sight, but I do the best I can by estimating where the column was and calling for "area fire," which I keep up for about twenty minutes. I never learn the results of this firing.

I receive quite a shock when the first light of dawn reveals a dead German soldier stretched out on the steps about two feet from me. I now know the source of the unusual smell that persisted throughout the night. He evidently was killed by our artillery early the previous day. I have two soldiers carry him into one of the basement rooms.

Potts, my indispensable runner, radioman, and wireman, and I immediately set out to find the best OP. We go up through the badly damaged building and discover that none of the windows face the airfield. It is but a few moments' work to knock out some tiles from the roof so we can observe. Even from this added height, however, there is nothing to be seen; nothing moves on the airfield to our front. The rest of the day is spent relaying messages and fire orders from Lieutenant Nestor, who is observing fire at the eastern end of the airfield. Because Nestor's radio does not have the range necessary to reach our mortar position, I receive and relay his fire orders.

Earlier in the day, Nestor and his radioman, Private Frederick Riebel, went from position to position on the ridge at the eastern end of the field, observing mortar fire on the German troops in the valley to the east of the airfield. Despite the heavy German artillery fire on his ridge, Nestor finally found an exposed position from which he was able to see for miles in all directions. From this position, Nestor observes the massing of several battalions of German infantry preparing to attack our battalion's tenuous hold on the airfield. Realizing at once the importance of his target, he calls for artillery fire and promises to observe. Every few minutes he increases the number of enemy troops to his front as his observations reveal more and more units collecting in the valley.

Word for word I repeat his observations and commands into my radio mouthpiece and relay the answers from the artillery back to Nestor. As his continuing observations reveal the size and importance of his target, more and more artillery is promised. "Will fire 3 battalions," I relay from the artillery to Nestor. A few minutes later, "Will fire 6 battalions" is the message. "I want TOT, Price," Nestor says. "Tell them I want a TOT!" And TOT, or "time on target," which means that a large number of artillery battalions time the exact instant their guns fire so that their shells reach the target at the same time, is exactly what is needed. Soon, word comes that sixteen battalions of artillery will fire a TOT on our target.

At last the awaited message comes: "TOT on the way!" Miles to our rear we hear the firing of battalion after battalion of artillery. Suddenly the air overhead is full of the swishing and slithering noise of the shells. And then, beyond the edge of the airfield, after a moment of deathly silence, we hear the mighty roar of dozens of artillery shells exploding at the same instant.

"Right in there!" Nestor yells. "That's it! They're running all over the place. Repeat the fire! Repeat it!" And repeated it is. For the next half an hour, Nestor continues to direct the firing, shifting the shells from one part of the valley to the other, wherever he sees the shattered German forces. And then suddenly, in the midst of a fire order from Nestor, I hear a loud click, then silence. Utter silence. Days later I learn what happened: Nestor's radio silence was caused by an enemy artillery shell bursting just a few feet over his position. Nestor and Riebel were showered with a deadly hail of shell fragments, severely wounding both.

Nestor's foot was almost severed, and Riebel received several wounds that proved to be fatal. But they accomplished their mission. The German counterattack was shattered, and no further attempt was made to recapture our position. Lieutenant Nestor was later awarded the Distinguished Service Cross for this action.

A few hours later, L Company is ordered to rejoin the rest of the battalion at the eastern edge of the airfield in anticipation of another counterattack. We march along the edge of the airfield in the dark. In all directions we hear the continuous rumble of artillery fire. Now Jerry begins to throw shells at our column. How do they know we are here? We dive into the ditches alongside the road. The word passes along the line that there are casualties up ahead.

We move on, and the intensity of the incoming artillery fire heightens. At the end of the airfield, we move off to the right a few hundred yards, and the company begins digging in. The ground here is fairly level and seems, in the dark, to be alternating open farm fields and small woods with sparse vegetation. My radioman and I begin to dig in with the company command post personnel. It is too dark to observe. I will move to the front at daylight. We try to sleep in the muddy hole. Each incoming salvo of shells awakens us, but most seem to be falling to our rear.

The next morning, the twentieth of March, after eating a cold K ration, Potts and I move forward to find an observation post. We skirt a small, open field on our left and enter a small woods. At the far end of the woods is the front line. I can see a few riflemen to the right and left lying in the very shallow slit trenches.

We move to the edge of the woods, and I find that there are several large fields in front of us, with small hedges lining them.

The ground rises to the front, and I realize that I will not be able to make long-range observations as I can not see over the rise ahead of me. Nevertheless, here we are, and here we will stay. Potts busies himself in starting a slit trench, while I study the terrain to the front. A dirt road runs into our front from the direction of the enemy just to my left. I mentally note this as a good route for the enemy to use if they attack.

"Lieutenant, I've hit water and I've only dug six inches!" Potts mutters. "Well, keep digging," I reply. "We may need it before long." The words are hardly out of my mouth when we hear the swish of incoming shells. The Germans have marked the range to the edge of the woods exactly. Potts and I dive into the little indentation he has dug. Potts lands on top of me. "Move over, move over!" Potts is excited. So am I. We huddle together as shell after shell shatters the morning. Some hit to our left, some to our right. After an eternity the shelling stops. Now Potts really begins to dig. I pull out my entrenching tool and join him. We enlarge our hole so that it is about five feet long and, including the dirt we throw to the front, about two feet deep. Water flows down the sides and collects in the bottom.

We try bailing with our helmets. Then we dig deeper, but still the water comes in. We now have the hole large enough for both of us to get into, but of course, it offers us no protection from overhead bursts. Potts and I spend the morning crouched by the side of our hole, ready to jump into it when the shelling resumes. I make a remark about our "bathtub," but Potts ignores it. Several times we are forced to jump into the water, as more enemy shells come in. "Where are they getting all this artillery?" I ask. Potts just shrugs his shoulders.

Suddenly the air is filled with the sound of an ungodly shrieking noise. It begins far to our front and steadily grows nearer. It is not one sound but dozens of sounds. "Screamin' meemies!" I have to yell to Potts to hear me over the awful noise. These are the German multiple rockets, which are launched in salvos and fall erratically over a tremendous area. You can hear their screech from the time they fire until they hit.

We are hugging the bottom of the hole. Our faces are pushed into the water, as we wait for the shells to land. Suddenly, the earth begins to convulse, as shell after shell hits and explodes. The thin-shelled rockets carry an enormous powder charge and cause more damage from concussion than from shell fragments. The first to hit sounds like it is just outside our hole. The rest fall to our left and rear. I guess that most of them are landing near the road by the airfield that we marched up the night before. We hear large fragments of the rocket shells humming through the air behind us. They sound like loose aircraft propellers. We know that these large shards can cut a body in two.

Now it is quiet again. I send Potts back to the command post to find out what is going on and to dig our sleeping hole at that location much deeper. Soon after he leaves one of our Sherman tanks comes clattering and roaring up the airfield road and backs into the edge of the woods about one hundred yards to my left. Despite the fact that I know he will add tremendous firepower to our defense if we are attacked, I join in the groans of the nearby riflemen and hasten back into the hole. The noise he makes cannot help but draw fire, and a few minutes later, as predicted, Jerry shells begin falling around the tank. Over the edge of my slit trench, I see the tank crew clamber aboard and slam the hatch cover down with a loud clang. I hear a rifleman from a nearby hole shout derisively, "I wish I had one of them portable foxholes!" I hear the tank engine start with a roar, and the tank backs up several tank lengths into the woods. Evidently, this trick works, as the shelling in the vicinity of the tank now stops.

Potts suddenly slides into the hole with me. He is full of news. He tells me that the command post is really digging in. "The largest CP I've ever seen," he adds. Then he tells me that one of the "screamin' meemies" hit a large dugout at the edge of the airfield road and killed everyone in it. And, he says, a rifle platoon of colored soldiers is digging in the field back by the command post. Each battalion will receive a platoon of American Negroes, and each of these platoons will be under the command of one of the best platoon leaders of the battalion. Potts tells me that the colored platoon is to be an extra, or fourth, rifle platoon, and that K Company will get the new men.

In a lull in the artillery firing, Potts and I move down to our right several hundred yards, where we can obtain a good view of the landscape to the south. I observe through my glasses for about an hour but see nothing moving. When we return, I tell Potts to go back to work on our sleeping hole. I walk back to the company command post at dusk, carrying the SCR-300 radio set. As I reach the edge of the field, now on my right, I hear the sound of several voices calling out. In the gloom I can just make out a large number of new foxholes spread across the field. It is the colored platoon.

I listen to the voices. Many shells must have landed in this area during the day, and they are keeping up their courage by calling out from one hole to another.

"Are you alright?" one calls to an adjoining foxhole.

"I'm alright; are you alright?"

"I'm okay; are you alright?" The sound of their voices follows me as I cut into the woods heading for my sleeping hole. I am glad the colored men are here; we can use the help.

I am amazed to find that the command post is completely covered by logs and branches, with dirt piled on top. As I crawl down into the dugout, I find that it is like a rabbit warren of small sleeping holes cut into the bank. Each connects to a U-shaped trench. Potts proudly displays our sleeping hole on which he has labored so long. It looks very secure from all except a direct hit. I congratulate him.

The next day, the twenty-first, I go back up to the slit trench. Shelling continues during the entire day. A few rounds, then a quiet hour, a whole salvo of artillery or rockets, and then quiet again. Several times fragments of shells whip across the top of my mud hole, but I am delighted to note that apparently we are suffering almost no casualties from the shelling—at least not in my immediate area.

In the afternoon I receive a message to report back to the company commander, Captain Schuler, and find that I have to crawl part of the way as the shells begin to fall in my area. Schuler tells me good news: we are to be pulled out of the line tonight. The 104th Division will take over our positions. He smiles wryly as he adds, "They say we are going back to a rest area, but probably it's just to regroup and attack somewhere else." I reply, "Every little bit helps."

In the late afternoon I go back and meet the incoming mortar observer of the relieving division. He asks me the standard questions: "How is it up here?" and "What's Jerry doing?" I tell him about the artillery and rocket fire, and the absence of small-arms fire. I minimize the dangers as much as possible. It is almost as though I am afraid that I will frighten his division away and the blessed relief will not take place. The new lieutenant, a tall blond youth, is all business.

He walks forward with me to my observation post. He is not favorably impressed with the water in the slit trench but immediately sets about his work in a businesslike manner. He sends his radio operator back to lay a telephone line from the company command post to the observation post. As we will not begin our withdrawal for several hours, Potts and I seize the opportunity to get a little more sleep. We are awakened by the noise of tank fire to the south. It sounds like a night attack. Suddenly we hear a high velocity tank shell screech over our heads and continue its way to the north, up our lines. Another round follows it, this one evidently a ricochet, as it makes an awful fluttering sound as it hisses above our heads. It seems to fly for half a mile behind us before its noise dies away. I shudder to think of anyone standing in the way of one of these armor-piercing rounds.

Very quietly the relief takes place. The new battalion takes over our lines, and our tired, dirty infantrymen assemble in small groups near the airfield road, waiting for the order to move back. Finally we take our place in the long column and march back to the airfield buildings. Here we find trucks waiting for us, and wearily we clamber aboard. I ride with M Company. We are together for the first time in many days. We drive through the cold night for hours, and finally the trucks halt in the single street of a small German village, somewhere to the rear of the autobahn. The town does not appear to be much damaged, for which we are thankful. I find a deserted farmhouse, which seems to have a whole roof on it, lie on a bed, and sleep the sleep of the exhausted.

Without warning, shortly before dawn, there is a tremendous explosion behind the house. Plaster from the ceiling begins to drop all over the room. Now another explosion. Whole chunks of plaster, the size of dinner plates, begin to fall. One chunk lands on my back. What in the world is happening? It takes me a moment to remember that we are in the rear area.

I grab my boots, slide my feet into them, and rush out of the house. Another explosion comes. The concussion is terrific and makes my ears ring. But now I can see that the flash and sound comes from a field in back of the house.

I rush around a corner and discover the answer: a whole battery of 8-inch howitzers is drawn up in a line about one hundred yards in back of my temporary quarters. They are firing, one piece at a time, directly over my roof. The muzzle blast is terrific and is slowly taking its toll on the frail construction of the aged farmhouse. With each blast I hear the tinkle of clay tiles being dislodged and sliding down the steep roof. Having determined that there is no danger, except for the whole house collapsing, I go back in. I see that no more plaster is falling, and therefore slip off my boots, cover my entire body with my poncho, and fall asleep again. Each time the howitzers fire they awaken me, but they do not fire very often.

The next day, I receive a visit from my old radio operator, Private Higgins, who wants me to pose with him for a photograph. I am delighted to see him, and after I try to comb my long, matted hair, wash the dirt from my face, and shave my week-old beard, we take the pictures. Later, a cheery soul sticks his head in the door and shouts, "Lieutenant Price, you've got a package." From behind his back he produces a cardboard box. It has been sadly battered and smashed, but nonetheless has all of the appearances of a gift from heaven. It is the twenty-second of March, and my Christmas package has finally arrived. After reverently opening each gift, I write my mother:

DEAREST MOTHER—

Guess what—? Not in a million years. I got your Christmas package today. Gee—it had been everywhere, and you know it was a great thrill to get it. It couldn't have come at a better

time. I was downhearted and very blue, as things have been
kind of rough lately, but here came the package.

Every man in the platoon got a couple of pieces of Nun-
nally's best, and did they appreciate it. And the rum kisses are
excellent. The peanuts I am saving for a bit. The toothbrush
was a reminder that I should brush my teeth once in a while, I
know. . . .

I certainly got a kick out of the wrapping, and it was just
like an old Christmas. Not really of course, because, well, we
were dragged out of the line last night and are in a Jerry village. . . . Yes, it isn't like Christmas, but the package helps. . . .

I don't suppose you have heard anything about our division
lately because we are always getting on the secret list. That
means doing odd jobs all over the place, . . . Jerry has lots left.
. . . The German people want the war to end, but the soldiers,
the old soldiers, are content to go on taking orders and getting
killed. We can lick them; we have, and we'll continue to. I
wish to heaven they would quit, as my nerves were never the
strongest in the world, but . . . we won't settle for anything but
complete abolishment of German military might. . . . Pardon
my soap box, but I have to keep telling myself these things.

On the twenty-fourth the mortar observers and heavy-machine-
gun platoon leaders assemble at the M Company command
post to receive another attack order. This time we find that the
3d Battalion is to move to the northern part of the bridgehead
and attempt to drive a hole in the German perimeter. The 3d
Armored Division is ready to break out in what may prove to be
the decisive action of the war, if—always the big if—the 1st Division can drive Jerry away from the main highway that leads to
the center of Germany.

At the German farmhouse used as M Company headquarters we go through the usual routine. The company commander

explains that we will move by truck the next morning, driving in convoy to the village of Oberpleis. Near Oberpleis we will dismount and move through the large town of Uckerath and launch an attack to the east and north. "L Company will lead." How many times have I heard that? "Price, you remain attached to L Company."

L Company's objective is a tiny village—Fernegierscheid. All units of the 1st Division are to swing their attacks beyond Uckerath to the north, trying to push the Germans away from the main Altenkirchen-Uckerath highway. We are to try to pin as many German outfits as possible against the Sieg River, which forms the boundary of the division to the north. Now we are issued our map sheets of the attack zone. We begin the tedious process of copying down the innumerable concentration points on which we can call for fire. We are told that the town of Uckerath is being attacked today, and that we will launch our attack just on the other side of the town.

About midmorning the next day, the twenty-fifth, we load into trucks and move north. Our route takes us back across the autobahn, and after driving through battered villages and alternating forest and following farmland, we pass through the village of Oberpleis. About one mile beyond the town the trucks halt, and we dismount. To the rear we hear the rumble of our own artillery firing in support of our attack on Uckerath, which did not succeed in capturing the entire town yesterday. Rumors reach us of fanatic resistance in Uckerath and the adjoining small towns to the north. Evidently Jerry is not giving up his real estate easily.

Potts and I take our place in the column being formed by L Company. As always, we march with the company headquarters group, just to the rear of the leading platoon. Already we can hear the distant sounds of heavy mortar and small-arms fire.

Ahead of us on the road the leading platoon begins to move. Soon we begin to march. The sound of firing ahead is sufficient to make every man maintain his five yards' distance from the man in front of him. I march on the right shoulder of the road, directly behind a Sherman tank, which drives in the center of the dirt road, and Potts marches behind me. We move steadily forward, up a hill and then down into a valley. Ahead of me I can see rolling farmland and beautiful tree-lined roads. The sun is shining brightly, and soon all of us are sweating freely from the heavy loads we carry.

I begin to take a great dislike to the metal monster in front of me. The fumes of its gasoline engine pour out into my face. I can hear nothing except the sound of the powerful engine. I can no longer hear the firing ahead, and what is infinitely worse, if incoming shells drop on our column I will have no warning whatsoever. I frequently turn around and notice that Potts is equally unhappy with the noise of the tank. Although we cannot talk over the roar of the tank engine, Potts is eloquent by the pained expressions on his face and the derogatory looks he throws in the direction of the tank.

Our march takes us across a flat valley. There is a field on the left, about two hundred yards wide, in which we can see German antitank mines. Apparently the Germans did not have time to bury them completely. They are camouflaged with dirt and straw but leave a telltale hump in the ground. As we draw abreast of the minefield, we see engineer tape on both sides of the road marking a small lane from which all mines have been removed and through which we march.

At this point we can see the church towers and rooftops of Uckerath to our left front. A heavy pall of smoke drifts over the town, and once again I can make out the sound of the fighting in and to the north of the town. We march without break, and now the road turns slightly to the left and begins to ascend the long hill up to Uckerath. At first the road runs in a depression and is bordered on both sides by bushes and trees, but about half way up the slope, the foliage ends and the road is again even with the surface of the surrounding fields.

And now that which I have dreaded occurs. German artillery, with almost miraculous accuracy, begins to drop on our approaching column of men. Because of the roar of the tank engine I can hear nothing until the shells strike and explode. The first shells hit the column about one hundred yards ahead of me. I can see the riflemen diving into the ditches on each side of the road. I dive also. Then there is a lull. Now word is passed back down the long column, "Move on! Move on! Get to the houses! Don't stay here!" Again the column begins to move, every man rising reluctantly to his feet and moving forward as rapidly as possible toward the supposed safety of the town. I leave the tank far behind. It has stopped for some reason or other, and I am delighted. Once again I can use my ears to warn me of danger.

As the head of the column enters the town, a salvo of four rounds strikes at the first house. I see infantrymen blown to the sides of the road like tenpins. We hit the dirt again, and then rise and move forward. Medics rush forward, and when I pass the shell holes in the road, I see three of our men lying there. The wonderful, valiant medics have already slit the trousers of one man. He is sitting up, his face ashen, watching as the medic exposes the wound and blood gushes down on the cobblestone street. It looks as though someone took an axe to his thigh. The column moves on into town.

Again and again volleys of shells drop into our edge of the town. We must be under direct observation from a German observer in one of the nearby villages still in German hands. As soon as each platoon reaches the town, the men break for the nearest houses for shelter. Now I hear the squad leaders and platoon sergeants and leaders encouraging the men to move deeper into the town. Gradually the units move from house to house, always on the run when in the streets, and then the word is passed back for all units to stay in the cellars until further notice.

Potts and I find that we are sharing the remains of a German watchmaker's shop with a squad of riflemen. The men notice the type of business from the advertisements and posters around the room and are soon engaged in searching for valuables. The shells striking in nearby buildings and in the streets outside are forgotten for the moment. There is a mad dash to the cellar as one man calls out, "I'll bet they buried it in the basement!" Soon the disappointed men emerge from the cellar stairs, grumbling that nothing of value remains. Evidently the German owner did a thorough job before he was evacuated to the rear.

I step outside the shop several times to see if the column is moving forward. As I look up the street, I see a storefront collapse forward into the street, accompanied by a terrific explosion and the tinkling of plate-glass shards. It is about five houses forward of me. Two riflemen emerge from the thick black smoke that pours from the shop, and one of them calls, "Medic! Medic!" I see our medics dashing from other houses and rushing to their assistance.

Almost immediately the word is passed from house to house: "Let's go!" And once again L Company begins to move forward through the town, from doorway to doorway. The column pauses, and I stand in a door. I see a combat photographer standing in the center of the street taking motion pictures of the column on our side. His uniform is clean and pressed, and his helmet is shiny. Where did he come from? The soldiers stare at him curiously as he continues to expose his film. Several call to him.

"Better get out of that street, Joe!"

"Another shell and that'll be all she wrote!"

"Smile purty, boys!"

Our column moves again. A medic tells me that two men were seriously wounded when the shell entered the storefront and exploded against the shop counter inside. Now up the street I can see that the head of our column is turning right on the main highway leading to the south. It is the highway that leads to the city of Altenkirchen, which lies some fourteen miles to the east. We are launching our attack on Fernegierscheid. As I reach the main highway I notice the body of a German soldier lying in the center of the road. A tank has evidently run over his body, as he is flattened like a pancake. His skin is yellow from the thick dust that covers him.

The column now leaves the southern edge of Uckerath and continues down the highway on a high ridge for about one mile. Ahead and to the left I can hear tank fire. We leave the highway and turn left down a dirt road that winds down into a valley to the east. At the bottom of the hill we march past one of our light tanks, which is burning fiercely, having been neatly pierced by German tank fire. The body of one of our tankers lies near it. A few yards farther and we see another tank burning. This has been a regular shooting gallery for some German tanker. We all have the feeling that the German may have us in his sights, and the column increases its pace on the exposed portions of the road. No one has to remind us to keep our five yard intervals.

Now the road turns abruptly north, and we are headed toward our objective. Ahead of us lies the Sieg River, and our job is to push Jerry back from the Altenkirchen-Uckerath highway and pin him against the river. The company commander directs the leading platoon to march up a long draw to the left of the road, giving us protection from observation. The road itself runs along the high ground, which is no place to be in a daylight attack. The second platoon is leading, and Potts and I now take our places at the rear of that platoon. I frequently consult my map, on which are plotted the various concentration points, and see that the draw will take us almost to the town of Fernegierscheid. Not quite, however.

We march up the wooded draw for about one-half a mile without incident, when suddenly, just ahead, I see white phosphorus shells landing in our column. The medics rush forward. The stench of the phosphorus fills the air and I can hear the burned men cursing. I grab the headset of our radio and call the mortar platoon. I suspect that these rounds are from U.S. mortars. Lieutenant Ciccone is soon on the other end. He tells me he will have the mortar firing stopped immediately. He is true to his word, and no more rounds fall. I send a message to Captain Schuler that the mortar fire was a mistake but has been stopped. I am furious that our own firing has caused casualties, but at the same time I realize that in a fast-moving situation the appearance of a column of unidentified men in the distance is sufficient grounds for opening fire.

Again the order passes down the column—"Let's go!"—and again the riflemen rise to their feet and move forward. I reflect that although the division motto is "No mission too difficult; no sacrifice too great; duty first," the division slogan ought to be "Let's go!" The former is just a bit wordy for the usual combat situation.

The second platoon moves forward a few hundred yards more, and the draw is now heavily wooded. Suddenly we hear the dreaded swish of artillery shells overhead. The shells just clear the top of the draw on our right, exploding on the ridge to our right. Now a second salvo comes in. Everyone of us can tell that these rounds are falling short. With a tremendous roar that deafens us momentarily, several rounds have dropped in the bottom of the draw, right in the middle of one of our squads. There is no doubt in anyone's mind: these are our shells falling short. Captain Schuler rushes to me. He is cursing me and tells me to get the shelling stopped. In seconds I am talking to Lieutenant Ciccone.

"Artillery rounds falling short! Our stuff! Get 'em stopped!"

Ciccone quickly asks, "What kind are they and where are they coming from!"

"Sound like 155s, and they are coming from due west!"

"Wait one, lad."

My call is unnecessary, however, as our field artillery forward observer has been registering his pointed complaints back to his artillery battalion. The artillery communications system is so arranged that any battalion can talk to other battalions in an instant. At any rate, the next salvo of shells passes high overhead, and no more rounds fall on our troops. I can see our medics at work on three pitiful cases lying in a row at the bottom of the draw. L Company moves forward again.

A few hundred yards more, and then to our front, the sound of a German machine gun breaks the silence. The leading scouts of the second platoon have been taken under fire. We are now opposite the town of Fernegierscheid, and all that lies between us and the town is a broad stretch of open field, about three hundred yards across. The second platoon spreads out along the edge of a point of woods that juts out into the field. Potts and I rush forward to the tree line and see that the riflemen are digging in since a rise in the field in front of them prevents any sight of the enemy. On our left the German machine gun is firing steadily in our direction. Bullets whip and crack through the leaves high above our heads. One of our light machine guns opens fire on our left.

I hear Captain Schuler ordering the first platoon into position on the right of the second platoon. Then he orders the heavy-machine-gun platoon to support the first platoon. I see these two units move out, following a slight fold in the ground which leads across the open field to my right. Although I can not see the village, which is hidden in a valley just beyond the field, I decide that I can support the attack by dropping rounds in the vicinity of the village, and at the point from which the machine gun fired. I quickly call for mortar fire using the concentration number plotted in the center of the village. The 81s answer me with gratifying swiftness. I judge from the sound of the first round that it fell just beyond the town, and I shorten the range by one hundred yards and call for area fire. The crump of the mortar shells makes a satisfying sound as one after another explodes unseen in front of me.

Now I see that the second platoon is moving forward across the field leading up to the crest of the hill. On the right I hear the sound of intense rifle and machine-gun fire. One of the machine guns on the right sounds like a German. The riflemen in front of me are advancing steadily. There is no more fire from the left. I help Potts to get the radio on his back, and we move forward behind the line of riflemen. Suddenly, I see the men ahead hit the ground at the same time. A machine gun directly ahead has begun to fire in our direction. I can tell that the bullets are going high above our heads, and so we continue to move forward. On reaching the crest of the open field I can see that our riflemen have reached the dirt road that leads sharply down into the village. The rooftops are just visible in the valley.

Now I see the source of the machine-gun fire: a gigantic German Tiger tank has moved up out of the village and placed itself at a bend in the dirt road. Its fire covers the entire road and much of the fields on both sides. Our men, now in the sunken road, are caught like rats in a trap. I hear the swoosh and immediate sharp explosions of bazooka fire against the tank. Some brave men are trying to knock the tank out with their small anti-tank rockets. The tank, which is so huge it fills the entire road, continues to move forward.

I drop behind a bush near the road and, grabbing the headset of the radio, call for fire. I drop the range another one hundred yards from my last firing, satisfied that the round will fall extremely near the tank's position. Now I am startled to see that the men in the road have suddenly started running to the rear. They are soon joined by all of the other members of the second platoon. I can see their faces as they pass me. There is a look of terror in their eyes, and they do not heed my shouts to stop. I am fighting mad! I want to get that huge tank, and I am furious at the senseless German resistance. Still, I cannot blame the men for running. I hear some of them yelling that the bazooka rounds just bounce off the tank's sides, that nothing can stop it. I know that our bazookas were developed to defeat a much smaller German tank than this monster.

Potts is pulling at my sleeve. "Let's get out of here, Lieutenant!" I see the sense in his suggestion, and we crawl backward a few yards, then get to our feet and begin trotting to the rear. After I have taken a few steps I realize that I must stay near enough to direct accurate fire on the tank, and I drop to the ground behind a small bush. Potts drops beside me, and soon I am on the radio.

"Right five-zero! One round heavy!" I know that only a hit from the delayed-fuse heavy rounds will do any good.

"On the way!" My radio is working perfectly.

The rounds strike in the exact position where I last heard the tank. "Repeat!" I say. "Five rounds heavy!"

"On the way!" I can hear the click in my earphone as the mortars, somewhere in the rear, fire. There are five clicks. Now the wait, and then, one after another, the rounds are falling in the roads. One of the explosions seems to include the sound of a metallic clang. Maybe I hit the bastard!

For the first time I am aware that Potts is screaming at me. "Get your head down!" I have been sitting on the ground, looking through my field glasses in all directions. Potts shouts again, "They're going right over your helmet! Get your head down!" I take the glasses away from my eyes and see that the stream of tracer bullets from the tank machine gun is passing inches above my head. I drop to the ground, still determined to stop the tank. A moment later the muffled roar of the tank engine stops and its machine gun stops firing. Now I can hear our machine guns and rifle fire on the right, where the first platoon and the "heavies" are keeping up the fire.

I have done the best I can against the tank, and so I signal Potts to move back to the rear, and soon we are turning back across the field to the edge of the trees. As we arrive I can see that there is no disorder and the men are grimly digging in to hold their position. I find Captain Schuler and report that the tank has stopped firing. The firing on the right has also come to a stop, and Captain Schuler orders the company to move forward once again against the village. Now the long line of riflemen begin their wary advance, every man crouched low and momentarily expecting enemy fire. None comes, however, and soon the leading riflemen are signaling the men behind them to come forward.

I pause at the huge Tiger tank. Its right track, which is about three feet wide, has been broken just at the right front of the machine. Evidently my heavy mortar round did the trick. I can see the marks made by the exploding bazooka rounds on the turret and side of the tank, and can see that no penetration of the thick armor resulted. The turret hatch is open; apparently the tankers, finding that they were immobilized, deserted their vehicle and departed for the rear.

It is dusk. I move on down the last fifty yards into the village and look at the destruction wrought by the artillery fire and my mortar rounds. The Germans have pulled back . . . and there is no resistance. Potts and I wearily move into a house that is serving as the company command post. Here I am told that my friend, Sergeant Atkins, of the heavy-machine-gun platoon, was shot through the head as the second platoon was attacked by German troops. But one of his machine gunners tells me that Atkins was alive when he was taken to the rear. It is not until the war's end that I discover he was hit by a bullet that went in one cheek and out the other and miraculously recovered from his wound.

Captain Schuler explains the plan of attack for the next day, and then we all find a bed or a spot on a floor and fall into exhausted sleep. During the early part of the night I am awakened by a roar far to the south. It is the sound of hundreds of motors moving steadily to the east. Then it dawns on us that this is the breakthrough. The 3d Armored Division is smashing down the highway to Altenkirchen. We listen with keen interest, but there is no pause in the roar. The breakout is a success. Remagen bridgehead is no more.

The next day we move out of Fernegierscheid to the north, heading for a small village called Mittlescheid on the bank of the Sieg River. The day is sunny and we march rapidly. Our route takes us through another tiny village, and just outside of town stands a complete battery of German artillery. Shells are stacked by each gun, and the guns themselves are painted a dirty yellow color. This is the first time we have succeeded in capturing German artillery pieces since I joined the division. It is obvious that the guns are in perfect condition, and they all point to the east, in the direction of Uckerath. German prisoners we find in the area tell me that there was no gasoline for the trucks to tow the guns away.

Later in the morning our column follows a small stream in a deep valley. I am startled to see a German tank high on a hill to the right overlooking our column. Although through my glasses I can see no signs of movement near the tank, I rush to Captain Schuler to point out the danger. He, too, examines the tank through his smaller set of glasses but decides that it is probably deserted. The column moves on, but I cannot help but feel the goose pimples on the back of my neck until we are out of sight of the distant tank.

Finally we come to our objective. We find that all enemy soldiers, except for a few deserters we find in the village, have crossed the Sieg to the north. The village has not suffered much damage, and we are delighted to find some excellent Riesling wine and German Cognac in a small café. The next day I sit at an outdoor café table on a picturesque terrace alternately studying the hills across the river for any sign of Jerry and writing a long-delayed letter to my parents. A copy of the *Stars and Stripes* is in front of me. "I see by the S. and S. that we are off the secret list at last, so that I can say that we were in the Remagen Bridgehead and that we are in the breakthrough going out of it, and boy aren't we going great guns!"

I tell them a little about our dash from the Roer to the Rhine, and something about our crossing into the bridgehead: "Then a couple days ago the breakthrough. . . . We are thrilled and excited about our progress and the boys are beginning to get optimistic again, but not this chicken. Long hard fighting ahead, I'm thinking. . . . But at any rate, I'm well, and expecting to get home before 1946. . . . The Germans are telling their men that we shoot them, which is one of the reasons why they fight."

(Dom) Butgenbach, Belgium. December 1944. One of the tanks of the 1st Battalion, 26th Infantry, 1st Division, left behind by the Germans when they tried to break through American lines in Belgium. The U.S. medium tank (tank destroyer) in the center of the photo guards the sector against further attempts at a breakthrough by the Nazis.

U.S. Army, McCormick Research Center of the First Division Museum at Cantigny

First Division Infantrymen move up to cut off German counterthrust that threatened Büllingen, Belgium.

U.S. Army, McCormick Research Center of the First Division Museum at Cantigny

Left to right: PFC Phillip Graham, Bronx, N.Y.; William Phillips, Los Angeles, Calif.; and PFC William Berthold, Sheppton, Pa. Members of the 1st Division, 3rd Battalion, 26th Infantry examine a German supply container, 30 January 1945.

U.S. Army, McCormick Research Center of the First Division Museum at Cantigny

Infantrymen preparing to move on Soller, Germany, rest amid brush and foxholes until the artillery barrage ceases. 27 February 1945.
U.S. Army, McCormick Research Center of the First Division Museum at Cantigny

Infantrymen of the 1st Division cross over the Erft River on a tread-way bridge built two hours earlier. Bliesheim, Germany, 5 March 1945.
U.S. Army, McCormick Research Center of the First Division Museum at Cantigny

Troops of the 1st Division move out of Bliesheim to attack enemy positions in woods just outside of town. The tank in the foreground is a new U.S. medium tank. 5 March 1945.

U.S. Army, McCormick Research Center of the First Division Museum at Cantigny

First Division troops load onto a landing craft vehicle personnel (LCVP) to cross the Rhine River and reinforce the bridgehead near Scheuren, Germany. 15 March 1945.

U.S. Army, McCormick Research Center of the First Division Museum at Cantigny

A tank leads the way as infantrymen of the 1st Division advance on Scharfenberg, Germany, on 2 April 1945.

U.S. Army, McCormick Research Center of the First Division Museum at Cantigny

The author in Braun-
lage in the Harz
Mountains, 1945.
Photo by Ollie Potts

The author and his friend Lieutenant Grogan, 1945. Both had just
climbed to the top of Brocken and back down again.

8

THE ROSE POCKET

In late March we move south again to meet our truck column, which will take us to the east. We are to follow the armored breakthrough, moving, our instructions tell us, far and fast. The "big picture" is explained to us. The British and the U.S. Ninth Army have crossed the Rhine north of the Ruhr area, and we are to cut off the German forces in the Ruhr by circling east and then north. Far to the northeast we are to meet the British and our Ninth Army, completing the encirclement.

We clamber onto our trucks, and the dash begins. We turn onto the main highway to Altenkirchen, and the convoy rolls quickly through beautiful countryside. We pass many reminders of war: the wreckage of a German convoy, its trucks and motorcycles still burning; unburied German soldiers dotting the roadside; one of our tanks, standing disabled near the road; a German motorcycle with a dead passenger still sitting in the sidecar.

We are all aware that armored columns do not take the

time to clear the countryside and that we may be hitting resistance at any time. I feel quite exposed, sitting high on a truck traveling down a highway that may be again in enemy hands. As soon as this thought crosses my mind, I hear the sound of artillery fire far to the front. A few minutes later the truck I am in passes slowly by one of our jeeps, which has been destroyed by an artillery shell. The shell landed and exploded just at the side of the vehicle, and the jeep is riddled with large and small holes. A dead soldier is slumped in the front seat. And the medics are hard at work on some other soldiers by the side of the road. To the left, I see riflemen rushing across the field into a forest, searching for the source of the shell. Our column moves on without pause.

Miles roll by, and then, in the distance, the city of Altenkirchen appears. We roll steadily into the town, and see the usual examples of the destruction caused by air raids. I am once again impressed with the difference between the ruins left by aircraft and by artillery fire. Aerial bombing seems to leave many walls standing, the interiors of the houses either burned out or collapsed, whereas artillery fire seems to cause total destruction of most of the houses. Artillery fire also seems to churn the rubble into ghastly patterns, as there are more shell holes and gashes in walls.

We drive into the center of the city and find large sections that seem not to have been touched by war. Many white sheets hang from windows, signifying the desire of the occupants to avoid further destruction. We unload on a street and sit on a sidewalk eating our rations. We are told not to leave the trucks, as a further move is planned. I gaze up and down the street and realize that I can see almost all of the 3d Battalion. How many of us there are! The sight reminds me of the terrific strength we have, which we so rarely see in concentrated form. Now word is passed down the street: load up! We get back onto the trucks, and soon the column drives out of the city, heading northeast. The rest of the battalion leaves us to go in other directions. I follow our route on my maps and see that we have come about twenty miles when L Company's convoy comes to a halt in a small German town called Nieder Moersbach. It is surrounded on all sides by high hills, and I do not like the looks of things. Word is passed to me that there are Germans in the next town ahead, Steinbach.

I look around for elevation and select the tallest building I can see. Potts shoulders the radio set, and we climb to the fourth floor of the building. I find an office room filled with shelves of records. The room has windows that overlook the landscape to the east and south, the directions in which we are most vulnerable. I study the heights to the east in the direction of Steinbach but can see no signs of movement. Suddenly, below me in the street, I hear the sound of a German mortar round. It makes an unusually loud explosion in the narrow street between the buildings.

Potts and I rush to another room that has a window looking down on the main street. Below I can see frantic activity, as the drivers of several jeeps are trying to turn their vehicles around and move back down the street. While they are so engaged, another mortar round lands in the street. I can see that one of the jeeps has been hit, but there appear to be no casualties. The men in the street rush to take cover in the buildings. Potts and I rush back to the window facing east, but there is neither sound nor sight of any enemy weapons. No more rounds fall, and the rest of the day is spent in fruitless observation.

The next morning I tear a few sheets of lined paper from a German notebook I find in the room and, while observing for activity from time to time, write a letter home:

29 MARCH 1945

DEAREST MOTHER—

Believe it or not I'm writing this one while at work. I am set up on the fourth floor of a house and observing and at the same time writing. . . I wish I could tell you how deep we are in Germany, or where I am, but I can't.

Instead let me tell you how much I enjoy your letters, and how I wish I were home with you and dad—just loafing, drinking, eating, and trying to tell you a few of my experiences.

Yes, the whole story is long and interesting, I guess. Not very nice, though. I hope these fools will give in soon as we certainly want to come home for a while. . . . Tell pappy that we're doing fine, and I hope to be home by 1946.

Love to all. Pres

Captain Schuler sends for me. "How about taking a patrol out and seeing what's to the south of us?" I reply, "Okay by me, Captain." He asks me to check the high ground that lies just to the south of the town for any signs of Germans. He gives me one of his rifle squads, and I leave Potts to continue the observation. We cross a valley at the edge of town and climb to a high plateau with woods on the far end of it. I tell the sergeant to take charge of his men as he knows them much better than I do. He sends his scouts out to the front and follows a route I have pointed out that will make a huge circle and bring them back to the point where we have started.

We have gone only a few yards when the leading scouts signal. I walk up to them and see they are holding two woolen caps, the type worn by the Germans when not wearing their helmets. The patrol continues on its way but finds no other traces of the enemy. I bring the two caps back to the company commander, who is relieved that there is nothing in that direction. After thanking the squad leader, I go back up to the observation post.

The next day we move another twenty miles farther east

without incident. We pull into a forest by the side of the road to bivouac, and soon small fires dot the forest as men prepare hot meals from their C rations. The following day, after the company commander has given the officers the route we are to follow, we load onto the trucks again. On this day we are turning due north and will be in the back of the pocket. We now call it the "Rose Pocket" in honor of Major General Rose, who was killed while leading his 3d Armored Division in the attack.

I follow our route on my map: Wallau, Ludwigshuette, Eila Battenberg, Battenfeld, Allendorf. The miles pass. German civilians stand on the streets in many towns, glumly watching our convoy roll by. Liesborn, Hesborn, Hillershausen, Lengefeld, Lelbach. The land is hilly, and much of it is covered with small forests. The roads usually run in the valleys. Fichtdorf, Adorf, and the larger town of Nieder Marsberg. Finally, after a ride of more than thirty miles, we arrive at our destination, the little town of Wunnenberg. Here we receive orders for the next day. Our objective is the large town of Ruethen, which stands on high ground just on the edge of the Ruhr pocket. We are told that enemy attacks will most likely come from the west, as German units probably will try to fight their way out of the pocket. We will move into Ruethen from the north. No resistance is expected.

It is the first of April, and the battalion moves out in its truck column. We drive northwest to the town of Bueren, which was captured the preceding day. The usual white sheets and flags hang from the windows of the town. Now the column turns southwest for another eight miles, and we pass through the village of Hemmern. Ruethen lies about two miles to the south. We are entering from the north, as the other three sides of the town are surrounded by deep valleys. Our route takes us over flat, open farmland.

The column comes to an abrupt halt; simultaneously, I hear

the sound of rifle fire to the front of the column. Everyone jumps from the trucks into the ditches at the side of the road. Ahead of me the firing grows as automatic rifles and machine guns add to the roar. A runner from Captain Schuler races down the road, shouting my name. "Captain Schuler wants you up front." Potts and I move forward along the truck column on the road and continue toward the firing, which seems to be centered in the houses at the outskirts of the town. We pass squad after squad of men, all crouching or lying down at the sides of the road. As we near the first houses of the town, we crouch lower and lower. Bullets begin to crack through the air above our heads. "Watch out for snipers," a rifleman warns us.

On the left we can see groups of men rushing across to another street on our left. Now we come to the gate of the town. I can see that the Germans have constructed a huge log barricade between two stone towers that form the gateway. The logs are splintered and cracked from our fire but remain in place. Ahead of me I hear the steady fire of machine guns and rifles as the troops fight from house to house. To our left we can hear the crack of a sniper's rifle firing in our direction. Now Potts and I come to an open field on our left. We crouch for a moment beside a wooden fence that borders the field. Again the riflemen lying along the road warn us of snipers on the left. "Don't go past that field, Lieutenant."

However, I know that I must get to the front as fast as possible, and so when we get to a break in the fence, where there is no cover for about ten yards, I send Potts across the gap, telling him to run as fast as possible. He hesitates only a second, and then he is off in a mad dash to the comparative safety of the wooden fence ahead of him. As soon as he reaches the fence, I look once more in the direction of the house in which the sniper is located and begin my run. Although it is only a short distance, it seems like a mile. My heart pounds as I pass the open field. I throw myself to the ground beside Potts, and my helmet falls with a clank onto the street. "Well," I say, "we made it."

We move forward at a crouch to the first buildings on the right of the town proper. From here on all of the houses are built against each other. We move into the first house on the right side of the main street. Riflemen are crouched at the windows facing on the street. Again, they warn us of snipers. In the second house a light machine gun is firing from the doorway down the street at the second-story windows of a house that is located where the street divides to the left and right. I can see the curtains inside of the window fluttering and jerking as the bullets tear into the room.

Potts and I push on to the next houses. Sometimes we run out the back doors, and sometimes we dash from front door to front door. A sergeant sees me enter one house and says, "Lieutenant, we've got a bunch of Kraut officers in here. They look like generals. How about talking to them? They're trying to tell me something, but I don't savvy." He leads me to a bedroom of the house, and inside I see a group of about twenty elderly men, dressed in the gaudiest, strangest Jerry uniforms I have ever seen. I speak a few German words and the prisoners crowd around me, all trying to speak at once. I ask for the leader, and he tells me that they are not soldiers.

He explains that an SS officer ordered the town to be defended rather than surrender. The German tells me that every man who belonged to the fire department, the police department, the post office, and other uniformed services, were ordered to put on their uniforms and defend the town to the last man. The German assures me that this group has done no firing and surrendered as soon as the first Americans entered the town. In German I ask them who the snipers are. The leader replies that they are fanatical SS soldiers, but assures me that there are only a few.

"Well, what do I do with 'em, Lieutenant?" asks the sergeant.

"Send them back as prisoners. Let battalion worry about them. They say they're noncombatants."

Potts and I dash to the next house. Behind us another machine gun has been set up in the main street and is spraying bullets up at the second-story windows on the left side of the street. We find this house is deserted. I begin to wonder if we have not gotten in front of the attacking riflemen. Potts and I pause inside the house to listen for a few minutes. Then hearing firing again farther down the street, I step into the open front door of the house. There, directly in front of me across the narrow street, is a German officer.

He is as astonished as I am. I can see that he is wearing a camouflage jacket, and that his submachine gun hangs across his chest. For a few seconds we gape at each other, and then I jump back into the house, tugging at the flap of my pistol holster, trying to pull my pistol out. Just as I move, the German turns and runs down a side street. A second later I hear the sound of rifle fire from the house next to us. When I look out through the door again, the German officer lies dead on the steps leading into a building across the street. I thank my lucky stars that he did not simply swing his submachine-gun muzzle down and pull the trigger. I would have been cut in half at that range.

Potts and I continue forward from house to house, and gradually the firing diminishes as the leading platoons make their way to the southern side of the town. I find Captain Schuler, and he is confident that the town is ours. A squad leader rushes in to tell the company commander that a German child has been hit in the abdomen by our machine-gun fire. The soldier says that the child ran into the street and the machine gunner did not see him until it was too late. The child is being worked on by a medic but will probably die.

All resistance ends. The company headquarters finds a large house on the southeastern side of the town from which to operate. A continual stream of prisoners are brought to the headquarters, and I interrogate some of them. They all tell the same story: the German high command ordered that Ruethen be defended to the last, and sent SS troops to Ruethen to put the order into effect.

The headquarters group is desolate. One of two young company runners was killed by sniper fire just as he entered the town. The other runner is beside himself with grief. The two have been like brothers for a long time. I leave the second-floor bedroom in which the radio operators and the runner are sitting and go up to the third floor of the house. I dump my gear on a vacant bed and lie down for a moment. From the floor below I hear a muffled boom. It sounds like a shot, and I leap to my feet and rush down the stairs. I enter upon a tragedy. One of the headquarters men is sitting on a chair. His disassembled carbine lies across his knees. A cleaning rag is in his hand. Across the room from him sits the remaining company runner. The latter turns pale under my eyes. The soldier cleaning the carbine has accidentally pulled the trigger. He forgot about the round in the chamber.

The soldier is sobbing. "I didn't mean to do it! I didn't mean to! I didn't know there was a round in it! I didn't!" By now the room has filled with men. A medic rips the pants leg of the wounded runner, and I see a small round hole in the top of his thigh where the bullet entered. A thin trickle of blood runs down the side of his thigh. The runner gets paler by the moment.

Someone is sent to get a litter jeep. A medic pours sulfa powder in the wound and binds a first-aid dressing around it. But the wounded man holds his abdomen and complains of pain. A stretcher is brought in, and the poor lad is carefully placed on it and covered with blankets. As he is carried from the room, I can see that his face is turning the yellowish green color of impending death.

Later a medic arrives and says that the runner is dead. The medical officer found that the bullet ranged up his thigh and was deflected up into his abdomen by the pelvis bone. He died of the internal hemorrhage. His death casts a pall of sadness over everyone. To lose both of these lighthearted, devoted boys in one day is almost too much for us.

I find Potts, and we leave to find an observation post from which to defend our position. I spot a tall, concrete water tower on the edge of the town, not too far from company headquarters. We break open the lock of a fence around the tower and enter through an iron door. A circular staircase leads to the top of the tower, which is about four stories high, and there are small windows completely around a narrow gallery at the top. I can see for miles in all directions. Here is a perfect observation post.

And now I begin my vigil, searching the heavy woods to the south and the valley of the Möhne River to the west for signs of Germans attempting to break out of the pocket. The scene is extremely peaceful and beautiful. I find that someone has painted the names of the towns to be seen out each of the windows just beneath the windows. For example, one facing to the north has "Gesecke" painted beneath it; the one to the south, "Brillon."

When dusk falls, we climb down the stairs and return to the company headquarters. On entering I find that the German families have returned to their houses from the air-raid shelters in which they were hiding during the day. As I talk with the headquarters group I hear the sound of marching men outside our house. I go down to the front door, and a sergeant enters. "We captured a whole mess of Jerry kids trying to march through our lines. Want to talk to 'em?"

I step outside in the dark, and a shrill German voice orders "attention" in German. As my eyes become used to the darkness I see that there are about twenty youths, around sixteen years old, standing in two ranks in the street. Another youth stands at the salute directly in front of them and facing me. Speaking German, I ask who they are. The leader brings his hand down smartly, and I can see that they are wearing the black, long-billed cap of the Hitler Jugend. The leader of the group spouts out his words in an arrogant manner. "We request permission to be escorted through the American lines!"

"Why?"

"In order to take our place with the troops of our leader in defending Germany!"

"What kind of soldiers are you? Have you ever fought?"

"No. But we are well trained and if you will give us back our weapons, we will continue."

I am amazed at the absurdity of his statements. This boy actually thinks that he is making a reasonable offer, and that we will grant his wishes.

"What's he saying, Lieutenant?" The sergeant stands by me, listening with curiosity.

"They want us to give them their weapons and let them go."

"That'll be the day!"

I turn back to the boys, who are still standing at rigid attention. "You are prisoners of war," I tell them. "I am sending you to our headquarters." I tell the sergeant to take them back to battalion and watch the youths as they march off in perfect step, under the watchful eyes of the sergeant and his men.

The next day, just before dawn, I climb the water tower

again. A few minutes later I can barely make out some Germans moving east through the woods far to the southwest of Ruethen. Using the codeword for the day, I encode the coordinates of their position and send it over my radio to the mortar platoon. The first round, a white phosphorous round, falls far short of the target. The mortar platoon tells me that I am firing at their maximum range. I suggest they change to "HE" light rounds, which will carry a few hundred yards farther, due to their lighter weight. Despite this, the next round also falls short of the Germans, and I see them move back into the forest.

Later in the morning, I see a group of German soldiers emerge from the forest to the south of Ruethen, and this time they are within range. Again I plot the coordinates, and send the fire mission back to the mortar platoon. My first round is very close, and soon I am firing area fire on the enemy. I can see the men hitting the ground through my glasses, and I watch as they begin to dash back in to the comparative security of the forest. I continue to fire on the place where they entered the forest but see no more of the unit. I am unable to tell if I caused any casualties.

The only other movement I see from this observation post takes place the next day, when I see a platoon moving across a field, far to the west. I am unable to make out the color of their uniforms at this great range, but nevertheless I call in a fire mission, adding that I am uncertain as to whether it is a friendly or enemy target. After a few minutes, I receive word that they are our troops searching the woods for Germans, and that ends that.

In the evenings I practice my German, talking to the family of the owner of the house we are occupying. I find that this family feels that the war was lost when we crossed the Rhine. A young daughter in the family is especially bitter that there was a defense of her town, which resulted in such needless damage and death. This same girl teaches me the words to "Lili Marlene," writing them down for me in my notebook so that I can memorize them. This song is as popular with our troops as it is with the German troops, and indeed appears to be the only contemporary bond between us. All else is bitterness and black hatred.

I find time to write several letters. On the third of April I write my folks: "How terrible it is when you are so far in Germany that the mail can't catch up. For the last few days we haven't been allowed to write, and didn't have the time for that matter. . . . All the armor can do is break through, and as usual it remains for the Infantry to clean up. And consolidate. . . . Say, Dad, I bet you had a hard time getting used to flushing toilets again. I'll bet I'll never get used to it, and I'll bet that after this mess I won't be worth a damn."

Mail finally arrives the next day, and I am deeply concerned to hear that my mother is ill and in Lawson General Hospital in Atlanta. I write, "What is this I hear? Dad tells me that you are sick at Lawson. Now I ask you, what kind of a deal is that? Dad is the one who is supposed to be sick. So you just hurry up and get out of that bed, and get well quick. . . . Both of you need a good long rest to make up for the unrest of the past hellish years."

The next day a horrible incident of war takes place. Just as I leave the command post to go to the water tower, I hear an enormous explosion on a small dirt road that leads into Ruethen from the east. I rush forward and see that a jeep has hit one of our antitank mines. Grayish black smoke swirls in the air, and the jeep lies on its side, its entire front end demolished. Two men who were in the jeep lie on the ground. Medics are already kneeling beside them, and another soldier is yelling for everyone to keep back from other mines.

I notice that the jeep is from another unit. The occupants did not even know that the minefield was there. I walk to the first man, who lies about twenty feet from the jeep. I can see that he is badly jarred but will probably live. The other man presents the most ghastly sight I have seen for a long while. It appears that his face caught the full force of the explosion, and the entire front of his face, from jaw to forehead, has been torn away. The stump of his tongue moves spasmodically, and he makes choking sounds in his throat. The whole front of his head is one great open wound. He struggles as the medics try to turn him over on his stomach to keep him from drowning in his own blood. Both men are given morphine, and gradually the seriously injured man ceases to struggle. An ambulance arrives, and we shout at its driver to keep him from driving into the minefield. I watch the pitiful cases being loaded into the ambulance, and then walk on to my observation post. How cruel fate can be at times.

On the eighth of April we receive word that we are to move the next day across central Germany to attack a German stronghold in the Harz Mountains. The news comes as no surprise. By now we feel that we will be sent wherever the resistance is strongest. I write my usual pre-attack letter to my mother. And, as usual, I make no mention of the impending move.

I find on rereading what I have written that it is a gloomy-sounding letter and decide not to mail it until later. The only mention I have made of the impending action is near the end: "Germany is about beaten but it is going to take some lengthy mopping-up operations by us. Therefore I probably won't be home for several months."

9

THE HARZ MOUNTAINS

After holding Ruethen against German drives from the Rose Pocket to the east, we take up our drive toward the center of Germany once again. As usual, the 1st Division is sent to the point of greatest activity—this time the Harz Mountains. We make the move by motor, and fast! The first night finds us at the Weser River near Höxter. There, I see five of our light tanks, standing equally spaced along a road, looking as though they are on parade. As we drive slowly alongside, we notice that each has a neat round hole in its turret or body. Some are burned.

I spend the next day, April tenth, in an observation post overlooking the river, and aside from being sniped at once from across the Weser, I have nothing to do but examine the headstones of the graveyard in which I find myself. After dark we push on again in a motorized, blacked-out column. It is pitch black, and terrifying. As usual, there are ten men to each jeep and trailer, and we speed recklessly through dense forests with only one thought in mind: keep the luminous reflector on the back of the trailer ahead in sight. Why we have not had a wreck is a mystery. At times our speed reaches thirty-five miles per hour, and the distance beyond which the jeep in front becomes invisible is only fifteen feet!

We continue driving through the next day, the eleventh, and have the pleasure of being bracketed by a German tank gun as we begin a long descent into a valley. In such cases, the standard procedure is for the driver to push his accelerator to the floor and pray. Not a vehicle is hit, but do not ask me why not! Late in the afternoon we arrive in Windhausen and Badenhausen, tiny villages lying at the foot of the Harz. There is a flurry of excitement while rounding up some reluctant Jerries hiding near the towns. The commander of I Company is shot in the belt buckle at point blank range by a small-caliber German pistol. The bullet glances off and leaves the captain breathless, but unhurt. In our briefing for the attack that night, we are told that elements of several German panzer divisions, and remnants of many other German units, have been streaming into the mountains for days. The Harz Mountains, the highest in central Germany, are the only defense position left to the German High Command between the Weser and Berlin. Thus, they have become a rallying point, and a good one. Although the Harz, an island of mountains in a vast level sea of plains, lack natural barriers on which to anchor the flanks, they are still a tough nut to crack. The mountains are quickly surrounded by the onrush of the troops on our flanks who are dashing across the plains to the Elbe, but this fact has very little effect on the fighting qualities of the German troops during the first week of fighting in the Harz. Again that cross we have to bear—unconditional surrender— works to strengthen the spirit of our opponents.

The die is cast. The 1st Division will attack again. And I learn a new type of warfare—mountain fighting. If you study a map of the Harz closely, you will immediately be struck by the scarcity of roads and the density of woods and forests. If you want to walk from Zellerfeld to Altenau, there is no choice of routes; there is only one road to take. Being quite as clever as the U.S. Army, and armed with equally good maps, the Germans also possess this enlightening information and thus know exactly where to defend. The days of being chauffeured at government expense are over for a while; our feet take on their real importance once again.

Another regiment has seized Bad Grund, the jumping-off place, and we motor to that point. We start our march from there on the twelfth of April. The scenery is magnificent. A winding, torturous road leads up and up, through solid forests of towering evergreens. At one hairpin turn the German demolitions teams have blown out the entire curve, leaving a precipice on one side and a yawning valley on the other. This presents no difficulty for the foot soldier, however, and we do not pause in our advance. At dusk we arrive at a large factory located in a valley about one mile west of our objective, Clausthal-Zellerfeld. Here the battalion stops to eat K rations, sends out patrols, and waits for the portion of a company that has been assigned the arduous and almost impossible task of advancing across the high ground to the right flank of our battalion. Our battalion commander, Lt. Col. Murdoch, assembles his officers in the large factory office building that stood across the road from the factory. Here he outlines the plan of attack (as usual a night attack) on Clausthal.

During the morning, as our truck and jeep convoy winds up the roads into the forests of the Harz, I hear something being shouted from vehicle to vehicle. Now the word is shouted to us from the vehicle behind us. "President Roosevelt is dead! Pass it on!" One of the men shouts the message forward to the vehicle in front of us. "President Roosevelt is dead! Pass it on!" The column rolls on, and now the men are silent. It is as though we have lost our battalion commander.

We finally reach the entrance to the factory, and we gather in a large room inside the building. I sit on the floor of the flash-light-lit room and listen to the reports from our patrol on the radio. The patrol reports reaching the edge of the plateau on which Clausthal lies. There is some discussion on whether the town is defended. The patrol overran a German field kitchen. There is small-arms fire in the distance, then silence. The CO turns to me and suggests to his staff that I lead a patrol into the town. My heart gives a brief flutter, but there is no time to waste. I get to my feet, and the CO begins to explain my mission. Just then another report from the patrol: "Blue Six, this is King Three. At checkpoint four. All quiet on the objective." No time for patrols. The colonel issues quick orders: the battalion will attack at once. Surprise attack. No preparatory fires. I quickly join L Company, which is already on the move. A few yards far-ther, we swing to the right at a road junction; the road left leads to Zellerfeld, the road right to Clausthal.

After marching as rapidly as possible to the plain's edge, we continue to march along the road straight toward Clausthal and soon meet and pass the patrol. I am about fifty yards from the head of our column and roughly two hundred yards from the first buildings of the town when suddenly the awesome silence is broken by the noise of a German light machine gun firing directly down the road toward us. I am certain that I see tracer bullets going between my legs, but no one is hit in the first bursts of firing. We dive for the sides of the road, and the leading squad opens fire. My radioman and I begin working our way to the right of the road and out across the field, which rises gently to the right (south). We find a raised mound of dirt behind which we take cover, and then I proceed to contact my mortars to call for fire on the town.

It takes what seems an eternity before I receive the message "On the way!" which means that the first round has been fired. Soon I am hard at work adjusting my fire on the center of the town, the silhouette of which I can just make out in the dark. Adjusting 81-mm mortar fire at night is not easy, as the sound of the explosions is quite deceptive, and the flash of the explosion is often hidden from view, especially in towns. At about this time, my company commander, Captain Nechey of M Company, locates me in the dark. Nechey is never one to remain far behind in an attack and has an alarming habit of turning up when you least expect him.

"Price! What are doing?"

"Firing mortars, sir!"

"What's your target?"

"Center of town, sir!"

"What was your fire order?"

"Area fire; right, three rounds per point." (This apparently complicated jargon means simply that your mortars will cover an area about 125 yards square by dropping three rounds at nine equally spaced points within the square. Thus, twenty-seven rounds from one mortar or, more commonly, fifty-four rounds from two mortars, drop in the target area all in less than a minute's time.)

Nechey, who was in the business while I was still worrying about passing final examinations at the Citadel, quickly, and in no uncertain terms, puts me straight on the correct procedure for saturating a town by changing my fire order to read six rounds per point, changing the shell from HE light (shells that explode on impact) to HE heavy (shells that have a delayed explosion, which in towns means that the shell explodes somewhere in the vicinity of the living room or cellar after passing through the roof and upstairs bedroom), and having the mortars continue to fire until told to stop.

From my position, I can hear clearly the German officers shouting commands and the sound of truck and tank motors starting. Our soldiers successfully overcome the initial German resistance at the edge of the town and proceed into the town, conducting the usual house-by-house, room-by-room search for the enemy that characterizes all town fighting. Once we have a foothold there, I cease firing and rejoin my company. After entering the town, my company turns up the main street to the south and proceeds with the job of clearing the houses. In the southern end of the town, we run into a platoon of entrenched SS troops that has to be driven from its position. Dawn comes as the last firing ceases in the town. Because we have no artillery available, the bulk of the German transportation escapes unscathed during the night. It is evident that we have attacked just as the Germans were preparing to move out of the town to the more rugged terrain farther east.

As soon as it is light, the morning of the thirteenth of April, and as usual without any sleep, I find a suitable observation post in the second story of the very last house at the southern end of town, which is on the road to the famous canary bird town of Osterode. During the morning, the Germans make several weak attempts to counterattack the town from the direction of Osterode using the road down which I am observing. At one point, I take the M-1 rifle from one of the men and assist in beating off an attack on the house by a small group of German SS troops. This is the only time during the war that I fire an M-1 at the enemy. I believe I come close to my target several times, but due to the ground haze, I never learn the results of my marksmanship. The most effective weapon we have to break up the counterattacks, however, is the 81-mm mortar, which I continue to use throughout the day.

The next day I gain the little-known and not-long-remembered nickname of "One Round Price." Although the story later appears in our one-page mimeograph regimental newspaper, the *Spade,* I am sure that the annals of the 26th Infantry Regiment contain no reference to this incident of war. Because I have been firing on this road and the adjoining fields for many hours, I have become fairly proficient at estimating the ranges to the various portions of the landscape. During the day, while firing at some Germans I spotted on the Osterode road, one of the soldiers calls my attention to a lone German running across a field about five hundred yards to the right of where my mortar rounds are dropping. The German falls out of sight in what appears to be a sharp depression in the ground. (During my visit to Clausthal in September 1953, I will discover that this pit is about the size of a small room.)

Risking the scorn of the soldiers in case I miss, but feeling confident of my observation and my mortars, I deliberately call attention to the fact that I am going to drop a mortar round into the depression. Then, after carefully studying the terrain again and making range and deflection estimates, I announce the new information over my telephone to the mortars, ending my command with the confident words "One round!"

I hold my breath when the mortar position replies almost immediately, "On the way!" And then, just as I hoped, the round lands exactly on target—in the pit. The German loses no time in scrambling up the side of the pit waving a white handkerchief, running toward our lines. Although I can not leave my OP to meet the German, I am later told that he has a mortar fragment in his arm and was completely shaken about the incident.

Later in the same day we kill two German SS men who

have crept to within thirty feet of our house. One of them is carrying a *panzerfaust* (German antitank rocket), and I shudder to think of the damage that would have been done if the rocket had been launched against the thin wooden walls of our house. Incidentally, the two Germans were killed by fire from the machine gun of an M-4 American tank, which took up a concealed position directly to the rear of our house. Another day that I am thankful for the tankers!

On the fifteenth, I finally get a chance to write to my parents. I am exuberant over the gallantry I have seen in our battalion and over our successful attack:

> Greetings once again. It is really a shame that I have not been able to write more frequently, but believe me, we *just ain't stopping!* We seem to have adopted a new unknown quality. Believe me, it is something to behold. The men are fighting with a grim, earnest determination. They realize we've got them licked and their thoughts are, "So you won't quit, huh? All right you bastards, you asked for it!" . . .
>
> As usual, the good old 1st Division is going where the going is toughest. And that means SS these days. They are just as bad as the Japanese. Fanatical is the word! . . . Had lots of fun yesterday, like a shooting gallery. Only trouble—twice in the last week I have been 42 hours without sleep and get sort of tired, but we're winning for sure now, and boy we are going to town.

It is twelve and a half miles from Clausthal-Zellerfeld to Braunlage as the crow, or should I say canary, flies. In 1953, I will drive the distance in my car quite happily in something less than half an hour. In April 1945, it takes us twenty-four hours.

After remaining in Clausthal for a few days, our battalion receives the order to capture Braunlage on the sixteenth. Braunlage is a rather large town located in almost the geographical center of the Harz. A health resort in peacetime, it is now packed with convalescent German soldiers. Since other U.S. units have been attacking into the Harz from the north and south, we feel that the capture of Braunlage will be the last of the fighting for us in this particular campaign. (How wrong we are!)

Since other elements of the 1st Division have already captured Altenau, a few miles to the east of Clausthal, we have no trouble for the first few miles. However, once we progress a few miles into the extremely rugged terrain, we find ourselves running into extremely accurate artillery fire. Jerry has occupied his time well. Knowing every inch of the ground, every turn in the road, he has carefully zeroed his weapons on the most vulnerable places. Much of the artillery is heavy stuff from extremely long ranges. I pass a complete battery of German 150-mm howitzers, which evidently fired until the last moment before the crew withdrew to the mountains. Lack of transportation and lack of good roads probably account for the weapons remaining in position to fall in our hands. Another reason for the German accuracy is undoubtedly the fact that they have cleverly camouflaged observation posts on the various peaks near which we pass. There was neither the time nor the energy to try to send troops up the mountains to dislodge these observers, and we had to pay the penalty for our speed.

But artillery is not the only problem that faces us. In midafternoon a German attack from the left (north) strikes our lengthy column almost in the middle. Charging out of the gloomy darkness of the thick forest that surrounds us on all sides, the German unit by sheer accident strikes the battalion headquarters, which on a tactical march of this sort does not look much different from any other part of the marching column. Armed with "burp-guns," *panzerfaust,* and light machine guns, the German force comes very close to cutting our battalion in half, although the force's ultimate defeat is still assured, due to its small size (around fifty to seventy-five men).

However, with the typical élan and courage that characterizes all of the fighting of our battalion, the attack is shot to pieces by the staff officers and enlisted men of the battalion headquarters before much damage is done. We rest for some time at the site of this action, and I am amazed at how well the camouflage suits of the dead Germans blend with the surrounding leaves, moss, bushes, and greenery. Indeed, so well that one would bet that the chief of the German camouflage service sent his artists to this exact spot at this exact season of the year to copy nature. At other times I have seen the same camouflage suits, I have felt that the colors used were a bit too bright and gay to effectively do the job.

During this pause the battalion commander decides on his plan of attack into Braunlage. Possibly he feels he can catch the German garrison by surprise; possibly he has been ordered to take the town that night; or, perhaps, he plans a coordinated attack from two directions. I do not know the answer, but the upshot of it is that the company to which I am attached is ordered to split off from the rest of the battalion, take a small road leading off to the east, which will bring us into Braunlage from the north, and attempt to enter Braunlage from that road. We reach the road junction around dark and begin our lonely march. The road winds down into a valley, and soon we find the road following the general path of a stream that runs into Braunlage.

We have not gone more than half a mile when, suddenly, in the darkness ahead of us, we hear the tremendous explosion of a bridge being blown. Our hearts sink a bit, because this means that in case of fortifications, or a determined resistance, we will not be able to bring our tanks forward. On we creep, almost on tiptoe, cursing under our breath any noise that we make. There is nothing like an advance into the enemy's ground in a large column on a pitch-black night. You never know at just what moment the darkness ahead will flame to life, and the suspense is nerve-wracking, I can assure you. Every sound of the night sounds like the cocking of a rifle or machine gun.

About the time we reach the blown bridge, we hear another explosion, this time only a short distance to our front. Another bridge gone! We push on, even more silently, but each of us knows in our hearts that Jerry has us spotted. A moment later, a third bridge blows, this time almost in our faces. And still we advance. Now, the forest closes in on either side of us. It becomes necessary to close up the column to a few inches between men. Such commands and messages as necessary are passed from man to man in whispers.

"Machine-gun section to the front of the column." Then another message: "Lieutenant Price to the front." Wondering what is up, I walk rapidly forward along the silent column of men. At the head of the column I can make out the form of a German soldier standing in the road with his hands on his head. That is it: another interpreting job.

A voice whispers, "Prisoner, Price. Ask him where they are."

Placing my mouth almost in the prisoner's ear, I whisper sternly in German, "Where are your comrades?"

The prisoner shakes excitedly, pointing down the road in front of us. "There! There!"

I ask quickly, "Where is your machine gun?"

"There! There!" This time his hand is pointed almost at our feet and just across the road. Almost as punctuation to his last word, the silence is split. A heavy machine gun, scarcely twenty yards ahead, opens fire diagonally across the road. A sergeant nearby makes a strange noise and drops heavily to the road. The rest of the column scatters instinctively to the woods on either side of the road, seeking what shelter they can find. I run to the right side of the road and begin moving slowly to the rear. I can not move rapidly; too easy to start a panic that way. I have to find my radioman, who remained behind when I moved to the head of the column. A mortar observer without his radio is a very useless person on an attack. Crawling over soldiers, stumbling over roots, bumping into trees I can not see, I seek Private Higgins. I repeat his name time after time in a loud whisper, and finally he hails back.

He has already tried to contact the mortars on the radio but reports that he can not get a thing. We try over and over, speaking as loudly as we dare. "Four Z, this is Four C. Over. Four Z, this is Four C. Over!" Nothing comes back except the faint sound of static. Either we are too far away or the hills and woods are baffling our transmission. "Four Z, this is Four C. Over!" Still no answer. Then I realize that even if we can reach them by radio, I can not fire my mortars accurately in the dark. With no idea of where we are in the woods, and with no real knowledge of where the enemy is, I can adjust the fire only by sound, and even that is a dangerous and extremely inaccurate thing to do. My worries on this score are needless, however, because we never get a reply on our set.

After the flurry of firing dies away, silence falls again. As the minutes pass, I begin to hear the snores of exhausted men unable to stay awake despite the fact that at any minute the woods might be filled with the crackling sound of machine-gun fire. Minutes, or hours, pass. I find myself slipping off to sleep time after time. Finally, the message is passed around to form on the road, and as silently as we came, we file back down the road to the rear. I later hear that a radio at the extreme rear of the company relayed our plight to battalion, and we then were ordered to rejoin the battalion on the main road.

A few hours before dawn on the seventeenth of April, we rejoin the battalion that is bivouacking in a small field about one and a half miles out of Braunlage. The battalion is to attack Braunlage at dawn, and I go to sleep under the kitchen table on the kitchen floor of the only house in the field. To get to this spot, I practically have to walk on the sleeping bodies of officers and men who pack almost every available inch of floor space.

The sound of nearby small-arms fire wakes me from my too-brief nap. On looking out of a window, I am amazed to see several German tanks in the edge of the woods near the road the battalion marched in on the night before. They were there the entire time but mistook us for German troops in the dark. The German tankers were all sleeping a short distance from their tanks, and when they awoke to find the field covered with olive drab uniforms, the braver of the tank crews attempted to reach their tanks. Had even one German tanker succeeded, he would have been able to slaughter a large number of us before our bazookas put him out of action. As it was, no tanker reached his tank alive. But I must admit that our marksmanship was extremely poor, as at least five hundred rounds of ammunition were fired during the three- or four-minute action.

Almost immediately following this incident, the battalion moves out. Instead of attempting to enter Braunlage by the main road from the northwest, the battalion CO sends us in over a trail which leads to the western edge of the town and takes us to the highest part of the town, located in a deep valley. Thus, we attack downhill during the entire action. I am near the head of the battalion when we emerge from the woods at the edge of town. Motioning my radioman to follow, I enter the tallest house in the vicinity and race to the top floor. The building is a sana-torium, and there are a few patients still in beds on the bottom floors. From the top floor, I have a magnificent view of the entire action and am able to watch the progress of the infantrymen working their way through the town below me.

A few seconds later, the air is filled with the swishing roar of German shells going by both sides of my observation post and falling exactly at the spot where our troops are dashing into the town, an example of the accuracy of German artillery fire. I do not see how the sanatorium is missed, as I watch salvo after salvo fall in the road junction about one hundred yards to the rear of my OP. Our casualties from this bombardment are heavy, but as suddenly as the Germans opened fire, the fire ceases. From my window to the front, I spot a long column of German troops on the southern horizon, evidently falling back to new positions. Although they are at the extreme limit of range for my mortars, I call for fire on them and spend the next half hour adjusting fire. Although I do not spot any casualties through my binoculars, I certainly hasten their march.

When no more targets of opportunity appear, I leave the OP and rejoin my company, which has cleared all of the houses along its route down to the main street in the town. We turn left and clear the houses to the outskirts of town, and there at the edge of town run into small-arms fire from Germans hiding in the woods. I call for mortar fire on the woods, and after a few minutes of fire, all signs of resistance cease in that sector. A short time later, however, a small party of Germans infiltrate the town a short distance away and manage to shoot Lieutenant Quam (a machine-gun platoon leader of M Company who joined the 1st Division on the same day I did) through both legs.

Our custom is to select a likely looking house for company headquarters and give the German family living there from five to ten minutes to collect their belongings and move out. The house we choose in Braunlage has a twelve-year-old Polish slave girl in it, and I give the German family who owns the house one minute to vacate. I am furious.

On the nineteenth, Potts comes to tell me that he has been transferred to M Company headquarters to do clerical work. I josh him about joining the "rear echelon." Despite how much I hate to lose him, I am happy at his great fortune. I have grown to think of Potts almost as a brother, and I reflect that he has been my companion since the day I met him on Elsenborn Ridge, the previous December. A few minutes later, Private First Class Higgins sticks his handsome, mustached face around the door jamb. "You know what they say about a bad penny, Lieutenant. Here I am again." I am relieved that it is my old friend who will be with me in the next attack instead of a stranger.

On the same day following our capture of Braunlage, other elements of our division capture Eland, a few miles East of Braunlage. Since the division has now captured all of its objectives, this, I believe, should end the fighting in the Harz. However, this assumption overlooks the fact that in our campaigning in the Harz, we have not overcome all resistance and have bypassed the strongest position in the mountains.

Brocken, or Brockenthor as it is called on some maps, has the unique distinction of being the highest mountain in central Germany. Less than a mile from its peak is a slightly lower peak, which is connected with Brocken by a saddle-back ridge. On top of Brocken is a high tower of about ten stories. This tower houses one of the key radar sets of the German High Command. Many of the German soldiers defeated in their defense of the Harz fled to Brocken and prepared a defensive position there. At any rate, after staying in Braunlage a few days, just beginning to enjoy life, the news reaches our regiment that there are

German soldiers on Brocken. Regiment probably selects the 3d Battalion because it is the closest unit to Brocken, which lies a few miles North of Braunlage.

And so bright and early on the morning of the nineteenth, we load into two-and-a-half-ton trucks and take the road for Brocken. We continue for some distance on the main road, then turn east on a small secondary road leading through the dense forest to the foot of Brocken. As the trucks pull into the side road and begin to slowly roll along the narrow lane, things begin to happen to the towering trees that closely bordered the road. Without any warning, one of the towering giants, slowly at first, then gathering tremendous speed, crashes down across the road just in front of a truck. The column halts. The men in the trucks, unable to see ahead, wonder what the delay is. But before long, a tremendous shout goes up as another tree begins to slowly fall toward the road. Shouts of warning go up along the column, and everyone dashes from the trucks. The second tree crashes straight across the body of a truck, which seconds earlier was jammed with our soldiers. Another tree falls, this time between two trucks, and this time we are not so lucky: two men in full pack are caught under the enormous trunk.

The panic of a moment ago is suddenly gone. Riflemen scatter into the woods on both sides to provide us with flank protection from ambush. Dozens of willing men strain to lift the massive tree a few inches so that their comrades can be pulled free. Others take up an aerial watch duty and shout warning when the wind strengthens enough to send another tree crashing to the ground. By some miracle, only the two men are injured, but both badly. There may be other casualties in other parts of the column, but I am unable to see farther than a few trucks to the front and rear.

Word is passed to the rear for the pioneer section to bring

up saws and axes, and the rest of us go to examine the stumps of the trees that fell. There lay the answer. Each tree was recently sawed through, only a portion of each remaining intact. The clever Germans, counting on a favorable wind to topple the trees, thus prepared one of the most original defensive weapons I ever encountered. It is obvious from the sawdust and condition of the trunks that the trees were cut only a few minutes prior to our arrival, and I dispel the notion that we surprised the Germans at their work of felling trees across the road for a normal road block. Had this been the case, the trunks would have been cut clear through, and some of the trees would already have been felled before we arrived. With willing hands and good tools, we saw through the trees and clear them from the road in about half an hour. And then we proceed as far as the road allows the trucks—almost to the foot of Brocken. I am attached to I Company, which is assigned the mission of climbing and seizing the lower peak while the bulk of the battalion climbs and seizes Brocken.

Now the grueling part. Although the lower part of the mountain is not steep, we soon encounter a steep slope, up which it is necessary to climb by handholds and grasping roots and branches. It takes us, I believe, something like four hours to reach the summit, although I am not aware of the passage of time. In addition to my pistol, ammunition, binoculars, light pack, canteen, and helmet, I also carry the heavy and bulky extra battery for our radio set slung over one shoulder by a belt, plus my grenade and map case. Climbing was no fun. Then again, I am probably the most lightly loaded man in the company, although my equipment is extremely awkward to carry.

There is no organization in the climb. We go on until unable to climb another step, then rest, and after a few minutes go on again. Sweat pours into my eyes, and all about me is the hoarse sound of panting men—slipping, sliding, scrabbling men. Shortly before we reach the summit, snow begins to fall, and the air, which was balmy at the foot of the mountain, becomes extremely chilly.

At long last we reach the peak, and there, to our great relief, we find no Germans. Almost simultaneously with our reaching the summit comes the sound of very heavy firing from Brocken on our left. There are loud explosions and a roar of small-arms fire. Through my field glasses I can make out nothing except the occasional sight of smoke coming from the tower and a glimpse of one of our soldiers crawling and pulling himself toward the summit. The firing dies away as suddenly as it began, and all is still. We radio battalion that we have reached our objective and encountered no resistance. We add that the firing on our left ceased. We are told to wait.

A few minutes later, we receive instructions to return to the foot of the mountain and begin the long trek down. We are glad to leave the chilly and gloomy atmosphere at the top. About half way down, we hear a resumption of the firing on Brocken, interspersed with the sound of heavy gunfire. However, we continue the march down, and the trip is enlivened only by high-spirited action on the part of Lieutenant Grogan, a platoon leader of I Company, who decided to fire his submachine gun at a tree while descending the slope. Due to our keyed-up nerves, this sounded exactly like a German burp gun, and many of us hugged the ground until we realized it was one of Grogan's tricks.

On the way down, we pick up two German soldiers, who give us our first inkling of what is happening on Brocken. The soldiers state that they were part of the Brocken garrison and deserted when their commander announced his intention of holding Brocken to the last man. By the time we reach the trucks near the bottom of Brocken, the situation on top of Brocken has evidently been cleared up, as we proceed to Braunlage immediately. It is only late that night that we hear of the bitter resistance on Brocken.

As L Company neared the top of Brocken, their spirits were raised considerably. They had not encountered any Germans, and it appeared that the radar station was uninhabited. It seems that the Germans, massed within the tower itself and around the base, allowed the Americans to approach within easy range before opening fire, and then without warning rained a hail of fire on the advancing troops. From every window, the Germans dropped grenades, fired small arms, and launched deadly *panzerfaust*. Since the fire came from almost directly above, there was little or no cover possible for our exposed soldiers. Finding they could not overcome the German position by assault, our troops withdrew to positions of cover and returned fire. At the same time our mortars opened fire from tiny toeholds they had obtained farther down the mountain. I later heard that one of our mortars slid backward fifteen feet from the recoil of the first round fired because of the steep slope on which the mortar stood.

But tanks to the rescue! Our mortar fire on the tower was almost completely ineffective due to the difficulty of registering the fire on the point targeted—the tower itself. A round fired at just a fraction of too much range would travel hundreds of yards down the steep slopes on the far side before exploding. The solution to the Brocken problem turned out to be our tanks, which fortunately had been ordered to attempt the winding tortuous road that led to the top of Brocken—just in case they were needed. And needed they were, for the back of the German defense was broken only after the first armor-piercing shells of the tanks went crashing through the walls of the tower as though they were made of paper. By staying safely out of *panzerfaust* range, the tanks were able to place their fire at any spot on the tower, and it was not long before the German garrison filed from the tower with their hands in the air.

In the first few minutes of the German ambush, we suffered heavy casualties. The fragmentation effect of the *panzerfaust* missiles striking the rocks with their tremendous detonations was a particularly nasty weapon and wounded several men. One of the rockets instantly killed Lieutenant Abele, a very close friend of mine and an extremely capable and popular officer. The shock of his death was intensified for me in that until the moment of hearing of it, I had believed that the action on Brocken was minor, due to the short duration of the firing we heard.

On arriving back in Braunlage from our mountain climbing, I write a letter home. About all I can tell my parents about the situation is somewhat pessimistic: "I believe today just about winds up the army that Jerry had in here. We have 'kaputed' them as we say. I can't tell you more about this pocket, except that it was hell some of the time, and we were "goats" most of the time. The climbing variety. And so I am now expecting that we'll take off soon for other fields. As it is, we are about 80 miles behind the actual front now. And I expect we'll get up there mighty fast."

The next day, with the fighting apparently over in the Harz, I wax philosophic:

Strange and mysterious is the life of the Infantry! Naturally, that calls for an explanation, and here it is. I'm speaking to you from a rather ornately appointed German bedroom. I am seated on a German bed, writing on a table. I can hear no artillery, and I'm drinking some cocoa I just mixed, and eating ration crackers. No, I'm not to the rear, nor is the war over. Just one of those breaks.

Perhaps in a few hours I'll be sleeping in the rain, though I rather doubt it, and perhaps I will be moving somewhere. But right now, this is solid comfort. . . .

My runner is out trying to find a bottle, and so I'm alone—quite an accomplishment in this army. Seems that the only times you find yourself alone is when you wish you had about 100 men near you, all armed with machine guns. But the cocoa is good, the crackers are tasty, and life, for the present, is good to me. From Rags to Riches.

. . . I shall have to admit that things, in general, do look good over here. The "big picture" is good. But the things that the people at home, that the rear echelons of the army, the politicians, and presidents will never know is that for the man in the front, there is no such thing as a good "big picture." It is very simple for us—either we are going to get shot at, or we aren't. As long as there is any German resistance, no matter how small, we are going to get shot at. That one fact remains, and all the prisoners and all the ground taken cannot alter the fact that there are still Jerries with food and cartridges—that there are doggies getting killed.

Along with the strain that constant contact with the enemy brings, there is a new one added now. The soldier has a sickening fear that, now that the end is in sight, he will be killed. It is a horrible feeling. A feeling as though you might be dying when there is no need to fight; a feeling that wasn't here when we were fighting for just another objective; when there was no end in sight.

This feeling is making the men cautious, but I haven't seen a single example of a man shirking his duty because of it, or hesitating to take a risk. This is truly a great army.

The fall of Brocken ends all organized resistance in the Harz. Although German soldiers continue to surrender in isolated spots of the Harz for days, we have no more fighting.

A few days after Brocken, on the twenty-second of April, I am ordered to attend a demonstration of our new recoilless weapons, which are being shown in Germany for the first time. The demonstration takes place near Nordhausen and consists of firing two types of recoilless rifles and one recoilless mortar. I am impressed with the flat trajectory and accuracy of the weapons but can not see their use in front lines due to the tremendous flash and cloud of dust they raise when fired. But I am even more impressed with the well-groomed appearance of the ordnance officers, fresh from the States, who lecture to us on the weapons. One of them, a general, singles me out for questioning, probably because I am the scruffiest-looking officer present. "Well, General," I reply, "if I ever had to fire one of those things, I sure would want a deep hole nearby to jump in!"

On my way back to the battalion, I help the jeep driver drink a bottle of liberated German Cognac and fire two unsuccessful shots from my .45 at a deer. Noticing the rather sardonic grin on my driver's face, I decide to chance all on one more shot. Casually tossing the bottle in the air from the speeding jeep, I fire one more shot. The bottle shatters into a thousand pieces, thank God.

"Purty good, Lieutenant," the driver says.

10

INTO CZECHOSLOVAKIA

On the twenty-third of April, the day after I returned to Braunlage from the recoilless weapons demonstration, we receive the
wonderful news that the division is going to move into an assembly area about twenty miles west of Nordhausen and go into an
occupation role. We have heard this sort of rumor before, but
each time it has turned out that our rest period has lasted no
more than a day. Nevertheless, the news is received with great
joy.

The next day I receive a message from my company commander suggesting that I organize a variety show to help amuse
the troops. I immediately get busy on this and move from house
to house, talking to my soldier friends and looking for talented
entertainers. I find that our men possess a great deal of talent.
My former radio operator, Potts, volunteers to play a violin,
which he found in the rubble back behind the Rhine. Also on
this day, I go with a truckload of soldiers to a nearby mine that
has a large shower-bath room. In the shower room I luxuriate

in my first bath since the fifteenth of February. (There were two other occasions when the unit to which I was assigned was able to go to an army shower point, but due to my forward observer duties, I was not able to take advantage of the opportunity.) Over the next two days, I fill my little pocket notebook with possible acts for the variety show.

Our pleasant stay comes to an end on the twenty-eighth with the sudden news that the 1st Division will immediately move out to attack the one remaining pocket of German resistance—in Czechoslovakia, about fifty miles to the southeast. We hastily pack our few belongings and mount up into the waiting trucks, then proceed due east until we come to the north-south German autobahn, and turn south on it. Several times during the journey we are astounded to see thousands of German prisoners marching north up the grassy center strip of the super highway. Our 1st Division units are using both lanes of the autobahn to move south. The only movement north is the flow of German prisoners. In places, the column of prisoners exceeds two miles in length. We leave the autobahn and turn east toward the German border towns of Hof and Rehau. Soon our convoy enters Czechoslovakia. We march into a small village where we spend the night.

The next day arrives, along with frequent snow flurries, which contrast greatly with the beautiful warm weather we had the previous four days in Germany. I am assigned to I Company and join them this morning. I Company moves out immediately to seize the small village of Neuberg. We have no difficulty entering the village and, as usual, I push forward with my radio operator to the highest ground I can find on the eastern side of the village to begin my observations. I find myself on a high hill overlooking the village behind me with good observation over the high hills of the Erzgebirge Mountains to the front.

I am elated with the lack of resistance on the part of the Germans and am complimenting myself of this fact when the silence is rudely broken by the rushing, swishing sound of an incoming artillery shell. In a few seconds my observation post is bracketed, a shell landing behind us and one in front of us. We throw ourselves behind an earthen wall cut in the side of the hill, and I find that we have been joined by an incredibly ragged elderly civilian. I wait stoically for the next artillery round. It has to be a close one, since the first two rounds so neatly pinpoint our position. Minutes seem hours. No shell comes.

Taking care not to be seen by the Germans, I turn to the civilian, whom I judge to be about seventy years old. I speak to him in German and find that he is a Russian physician. He is one of the thousands of slave laborers our units have encountered in the last month in Europe, and he is overjoyed that the Americans have finally arrived to liberate him. In German he says to me, "Come see the great Russian doctor's home that the Germans have provided me." He leads me a little farther around the hill, and here I find a crude shack made of old boards, pieces of tin, and tree branches. It is a hovel in every sense. I send the doctor down into the village of Neuberg with my assurances that things will be much better now that we are here. I also assure him that his services will be needed by the many refugees we have encountered in Germany. He bids me goodbye; it is the last I see of him.

During the rest of the day I stay at this observation post attempting to locate the German artillery position, which now begins to shell the village of Neuberg. As so often happens, I am unable to see or hear the German artillery pieces in the dense forests. On the next day, the twenty-ninth, it again snows intermittently. Each snowfall quickly melts and the mud deepens. I Company moves out to capture another village, called

Krugsreuth. We march into the village without resistance, and I immediately move through our lines to a new observation post. As usual, I begin zeroing in mortar fire on the likely avenues of approach to our front.

I call for white phosphorus rounds, which are the only kind that can be seen when firing into heavy forest. The white billowing smoke given off by the phosphorus round drifts up through the trees and easily can be seen by the observer. After firing at different points and making my registrations, I call for a round I have plotted to land about one hundred yards directly to my front across a small clearing in the forest.

"On the way!" The mortar platoon sends me this message by radio. In about one minute the round should strike the spot at which I am aiming. Suddenly, to my consternation, I make out a man emerging from the trees at the exact point where I have hoped the white phosphorus shell will land. Through my glasses I can see that he is a civilian, dressed in ragged clothing. He wears a black beret. Frantically I scream at him as loudly as I can, at the same time waving my arms to attract his attention. In German I shout to him, "Run! Run! Get away from there! Mortar shell! Mortar shell!"

I can see that he hears me, but instead of breaking into a run, he stops. I continue to shout at him; I do not want to kill a civilian! After what seems minutes, he at last seems to understand and breaks into a dog trot toward me. The moment he does this the white phosphorus round lands in the trees not more than twenty five yards behind him. The man stops dead still, takes one look back behind him at the billowing white smoke, and breaks into a mad dash to my position. As he nears me I hear that he is calling to me in French. No wonder he could not understand! I wait until he comes up to me. All of the nearby infantrymen have him covered with their weapons—just in case.

After he catches his breath I question him in German, and he answers in extremely broken German, telling me that he is a French soldier captured years ago who has spent the war in German prison camps and as a slave laborer. He asks me why I wanted to shell him. I do my best to explain that I ordered the shell fired before I saw him, but he is unable to understand me. I direct him back to the company command post in the village, and he leaves muttering curses at such a rude reception on his day of liberation.

On the last day of April, I Company attacks and seizes the town of Gruen. Again there are snow flurries. Now I hear the rattle of small-arms fire on the outskirts of the town. The company has some difficulty in seizing the objective. As I move forward, the firing ceases. From the center of the town I see a row of houses on a hill overlooking the town. I take my radio operator with me to the highest one of these houses, which appears to be an excellent place for observation. From the second-floor front bedroom window I find that I have discovered one of the best places for observation I have ever seen. To my front, the hill on which I am located drops gradually into a valley about one mile distant. On the hill rising opposite me from the valley, there is a heavy forest in which a division of Germans could mass for an attack if they wanted to. To my right I can see at least two miles down a beautiful cultivated valley with forest on all sides of it.

I have only been at this post for a few minutes when I see Germans moving in the woods to the right of the valley. I call for mortar fire on the position where I have seen them. My first round falls so close to their position that I immediately call for area fire. My mortar rounds plaster the area, and I see a few Germans running out of the woods into the valley and toward the town we occupy. Through my glasses I can see that they are not carrying weapons and that they hold their hands high in the air.

The day wears on, and I find no more targets. An hour has passed since I fired on the Germans. Then a messenger arrives from the mortar platoon congratulating me on my fire. I am told that the group of Germans who came in to surrender report that I wounded three of their comrades, who are still in the woods. The same unwounded Germans have been sent back into the woods to bring in their wounded comrades. Around noon I hear someone moving on the first floor of the building I am in. I listen carefully and am rewarded by hearing voices speaking English. I go downstairs and find that several of our soldiers are systematically searching all drawers and cupboards of the house. They say they are looking for souvenirs. One private seems delighted when he finds a cheap ring with an imitation stone in it. I send them back to their units.

After returning to the second floor I send my radio operator back into the village to find some food for us. He promises me he will bring something back. I continue to sweep the terrain to my front through my binoculars, but all is quiet. After another half an hour I decide to leave the house and move over to an adjoining house to see if it is occupied by our troops. I leave by a back door and walk only about thirty feet when I hear shell after shell striking the house I just left. Five shells have been fired. Again I cannot hear where the shells came from.

After waiting a few minutes to make certain the firing has ceased, I creep back into the house and climb the stairs to the second floor. I realize that I must have exposed myself too much at my observation window: four neat holes appear just below and at the side of the window. Evidently, all of the shells but one went completely through the house, entering through the front wall and leaving through the rear wall, before exploding on the outside. One of the shells exploded in the bedroom. Furniture is torn, pictures broken, and gaping holes dot the plaster of the room. A small baby bed covered with white sheets stands in the middle of the room, and in the center of the bed lies a large fragment of a German shell, which I find extremely hot when I touch it. After letting it cool for a while, I stick the shell fragment in my pack as a souvenir. I do not know at the time that this is the last German artillery shell that will be fired at me in the war.

The next three days are spent in the same area. I am grateful that no further orders to advance are given. On the first of May we hear officially of the death of Mussolini. The next day, we hear of the announcement of Hitler's death in Berlin. On the third of May we receive reports that the German army in Italy has surrendered and that Berlin is now completely in Russian hands.

This period of inactivity of course has the effect of making us all think that the war is over. Then, on the fifth of May, I am summoned to the Heavy Weapons Company command post to receive a new attack order. I attend this meeting with a sinking feeling in my heart. The company commander gives us some interesting news: the 1st Infantry Division is now a part of Patton's Third Army. We were transferred from the old First Army for this Czechoslovakian action. The company commander issues the usual attack order, and I make notes: "I and K Companies to pass through L Company. . . . I Company to attack to phase line 4. . . . I and K Companies to have one section of three mortars each. . . . Lieutenant Price will remain with I Company. . . . Roads extremely bad. . . . Mortars may have to be hand-carried."

I return to I Company's position, and after making the necessary preparations for tomorrow's dawn attack I, like almost

everyone else, find a quiet corner to write a letter. I decide not
to mail the letter, and when I finish it, I fold it and place it in my
field jacket breast pocket.

5 MAY 1945

DEAREST MOTHER AND FATHER,

This letter I will delay—

Tomorrow morning early we move out again. All day today
we have heard the reports of various units in this last remaining pocket surrendering. But the climax came when the SHAEF
announced that tomorrow at 12 noon the pocket will surrender. And yet we have our battle orders—we move out at dawn.

Can you imagine our feelings? No resistance met, however
light, ever fails to cause casualties. We now wonder, who will
be it tomorrow? Who will be the last killed, and secretly in
our hearts we feel that our luck has been too good.

I pray sincerely that I won't be the unlucky one tomorrow.
Not that they aren't all praying the same thing. The situation
map in headquarters—a few days ago so filled with pockets of
resistance, now seems blank. There is only one pocket remaining—our pocket!

And so once again, I pack the pack, get my maps, and clean
my field glasses. To you, sir, I again extend my admiration for
your life's work. [My father was a medical corps surgeon in a
field hospital in the Argonne offensive in World War I and com-
manded the largest field hospital of General Patton's Third
Army (the Eighth Convalescent Hospital) in the invasion of
Normandy. Shortly after D day, he was flown as an invalid to a
General Hospital in Georgia and retired from active duty.] You
should be proud. To you mother, the word is blessing enough. I
can only repeat those things I have so often said. You have given
me the talents I have today, and you have taught me courage.

During this phase of the march, I fire at a platoon of German infantry dug into foxholes. My first two rounds land well beyond the soldiers. I mentally note that the range is much shorter than I originally thought. I tell the mortars to drop their range by one hundred yards and call for another round. This time the round lands just in front of one of the foxholes.

I change my type of ammunition and call for HE heavy, which will penetrate several feet into the muddy ground before it explodes. This ought to shake them up, I say to myself. I fire about six rounds of HE heavy, changing the range and direction for each round, and am satisfied to see that my rounds land fairly close to some of the foxholes, although I do not score a direct hit. Shortly after the last round explodes, with its geyser of smoke and mud shooting straight upward for fifty feet, I notice that the flanking platoon of I Company has taken up positions in the edge of the forest to the right of the German line.

Now an amazing thing happens. I see that several of the Germans in the foxholes have raised their hands and are waving them. Not a shot is fired. And a few seconds later I see the German soldiers climbing from their foxholes without their weapons and walking toward our position. They all hold their hands in the air. We are amazed to see that the entire platoon of Germans, approximately thirty to forty men, have now formed themselves into regular ranks and are marching toward our position with a sergeant calling out the step to his men. Through my field glasses, I watch them approach and halt before an American officer about fifty yards to my right. I see the German commander execute a smart salute. There is some conversation going on. The German officer surrenders his pistol. Now five of our soldiers take their positions as guards around the enemy platoon, which marches off to our rear in regular military close order.

On several occasions during the march, we hear very heavy machine-gun, rifle, and artillery fire on our right. Some less fortunate part of the 1st Division is catching hell over there. The 16th Infantry is over there, too. Rumors begin to sift up and down the column that units on a road to our right are meeting very stiff resistance from fanatical SS troops.

The march continues, and the entrenching shovel, the full pack, the full canteen, the binoculars, the wet woolen uniform, the helmet, and the extra radio battery seem heavier and heavier. As in all attacks, the long column of men frequently halts. We stand in line feeling reluctant to sit down or rest because we know the column may soon move again. As often as not this is the case, and we move on almost immediately after we halt.

I write another letter home:

MAY 7, 1945
To continue the previous letter—

The *war* here is *over!* The war, I repeat, *here,* I say again, *here,* is—and I ain't fooling, *over!!!* Here's what happened today—to our part of the First Infantry Division.

First thing this morning we were called very early and on trying to put my shoes on, I found that I had swollen feet from the long wet push of yesterday. We had marched in mud, rain, and fog. So you see, the feet were sore. At twelve o'clock yesterday we listened on the radio but, no, the war went on. Heartbreak No. 1.

This morning we moved out again to do another long push and going down the wooded slopes we reached a valley. There we prepared to go up the other side and just then battalion H.Q. radioed for us to return at once to the positions we had left this morning. Our rifle company commander said—"Well, boys, the war's over!" and everyone started yelling and shooting rifles, automatic rifles, pistols, carbines, machine guns, and tommy guns, which alarmed other units no end. Sounded like a deadly battle going on, and one company thought they were pinned down and cut off.

We tore back on tanks and jeeps and then were told that we were called back because Jerry was coming with a counter attack. Heartbreak No. 2.

We dug in and prepared to fight again. But as the day wore on we kept hearing that it was over, and finally tonight we hear that Ike says it's over.

We are sweating out Heartbreak No. 3, which will be that the war isn't over, and that Jerry is still fighting. We are unbelieving after so many rumors, but we are happy as hell, and so I sign off—

> Your happy son,
> Preston

The following day I write another letter:

8 MAY 1945
Czechoslovakia
V-E day
Rejoice all ye nations . . .
Today is Victory Europe day.

A bright sun is warming the green fields, and the radio on the jeep peals forth bells from churches all over the world. We have heard Churchill's announcement often. I am once again at peace. I'll bet my blood pressure has gone down 20 points in the last two days. Of course you know the shooting ceased for us all of 2 days ago. The news reached us on the march to attack again. We are all thanking God that our company had no casualties during those last two days of hard marching, and bitter weather. I figured out the other day that I have been in 23 battles or actions. I consider myself very lucky. I have lost many good friends, but we have made them pay over and over.

Yesterday I was sent to Regimental Headquarters, in Kraslice, with a great group of officers and men, and there we wit-
nessed the raising of a small American flag on a pole in the
town square. Some of the civilians (Sudeten Germans) were
interested, but many just walked off. Our regimental commander (Colonel Murdoch) made a wonderful speech. He
spoke of our dead, and of our victories. Of the part the 1st
Division played in placing the flag there. He said that the American civilians are not familiar with the division that fought at
Oran, Kasserine, Gela, Troina, and Omaha Beach, but we ourselves know who has fought the war, and what outfit has always
been there in the emergency, and always doing a great job . . .
A bugler blew taps and it was over.

INDEX

Aachen, Germany, 75–76
Abele, Lieutenant, 182
airfield, 124–33
Altenkirchen, 150
Altenkirchen-Uckerath highway,
    136, 140
artillery pieces, capture of, 147
Atkins, Sergeant, 146

Badenhausen, 164
Bad Grund, 165
Battle of the Bulge, 38–73. *See
    also* Büllingen; Hollerath;
    Krinkelter Forest; Mürrin-
    gen; Paratroop Cross Roads;
    Siegfried Line
Belgium, 8–9, 71–75
Boich, 88–97
Botts, Seth, 45
Boyle, Thomas, 80
Bracken, James J. "Father,"
    27–28, 50–51, 80–81, 103–4
Braunlage, 170–71, 172–77, 182,
    185–86
Brocken, 177–82, 184
Büllingen, 20–21, 25–26, 47–51
Büllingen-Butgenbach highway,
    21
burp-guns, 170, 171, 182
Butgenbach, 13, 39
buzz bombs, 11, 24

Camp Elsenborn, 13

celery soup, 105
chaff, 24
cherries, 106
China Mail, SS, 1
Ciccone, Sam, 15–16, 17; attack
    on Fernegierscheid, 141,
    142; at Battle of the Bulge,
    44; in Boich, 97; demeanor,
    79; at Roer River, 77
Clausthal, 165–70
Clausthal-Zellerfeld, 165
colored panels, 113
Corley, John T., 13–14, 72
Czechoslovakia, 186–96

Drove, 88, 91–94, 95

81-mm mortar, 15, 16, 169
Eland, 177
Elsenborn Ridge, 16–33
entertainment, 28–29
Erp, 100

Fassbender, Pastor, 109
Fernegierscheid, 136–37, 140–46
fire orders, 167
First Division, assignment to, 12
flying stovepipes. *See* V-Is
food, 22–23, 105, 106
Fort Ste. Addresse, 7
Frankfurt-Cologne autobahn,
    118–19
French soldier, 188–89

German Fifth Panzer Army, 10
Gessner, Herr, 109
Givet, 8–10
Grogan, Lieutenant, 180
Gruen, 189–90

Harz Mountains, 162–84. *See also* Braunlage; Brocken
Heavy Weapons Company, 191
HE heavy, 167, 193
HE light, 167
Higgins, Jimmy, 80; attack on Braunlage, 174; on Elsenborn Ridge, 25, 27, 30, 33; photo with Price, 134; replacement of Potts as radioman, 177
Hitler, Adolf, 191
Hitler Jugend, 159
Hollerath, 69–70
Hubbard, Overton, 80, 84, 114
Huebner, Major General, 32

I Company: assignment to, 16; attack on Gruen, 189; at Brocken, 179–80; in Czechoslovakia, 186–96; on Elsenborn Ridge, 16–19
Ingels, Frau, 109
Italy, 191

K Company, 16
Kelz, 98
Kraslice, 196
Krinkelter Forest, 59–65
Krugsreuth, 188

latrines, 26–27
L Company: assignment to, 36, 39; attack of Büllingen, 47, 51–52, 53; attack on airfield, 125, 128; attack on Fernegierscheid, 136–37, 142; attack on Frankfurt-Cologne autobahn, 118;

attack on Krinkelter Forest, 59; at Brocken, 181; on Elsenborn Ridge, 16, 19; at Roer River, 84
Lechenich, 100–105
Le Havre Harbor, 4–7
Lewis, Jack "Sunshine," 34
Liège, 10, 11

mail, 29–30, 35–36, 66–67, 79, 122
Manelli, Sergeant, 103
map, 92, 96
M Company, 14–15, 16, 115
meals. *See* food
mines, 88, 92, 93, 161–62
M-1 rifle, 168
Moersbach, Nieder, 151
mortar, 15, 16, 22, 169, 184
Mortar Platoon, assignment to, 15
mud, 78–79
Murdoch, Lieutenant Colonel, 49, 165, 196
Mürringen, 59–60
Mussolini, Benito, 191

Nechey, Walter, 15, 84, 113, 122, 167
Negro soldiers, 131
Nestor, George, 20–25, 80, 84, 114, 126–27
Neuberg, 186–87
99th Division, 71

Oberpleis, 136
Osterode, 168, 169

panzerfaust, 170, 171, 182
Paratroop Cross Roads, 40
Patton's Third Army, 191
Port of Southampton, 3
Potts, Allie, 80; assigned as radio operator, 36; attack on airfield, 126, 128, 129, 130,

131, 132, 133; attack on
Boich, 92, 93, 94; attack on
Büllingen, 48, 49, 50, 51, 52,
53, 54, 57; attack on Fernegierscheid, 136–37, 139,
143, 144, 145, 146; attack on
Hollerath, 69, 70–71; attack
on Krinkelter Forest, 59, 60,
61, 62, 63; attack on
Ruethen, 154–55, 156, 158;
crossing of Roer River, 88;
en route to Steinbach, 151;
in Lechenich, 100, 101,
102–3; at quarry, 120, 121;
at Rhine River, 111; transfer
to M Company headquar-
ters, 177; in variety show, 185
Price, Herbert H., 29
prisoners, 41–43, 55, 94–95, 155,
159, 173

Quam, Lieutenant, 14, 15, 176
quarry, 119–24

recoilless weapons, 184
Red Ball Highway, 8
Remagen bridgehead, 113–48. *See
also* airfield; Fernegier-
scheid; Frankfurt-Cologne
autobahn; Uckerath
Rhine River, 109, 111, 112, 117
Riebel, Frederick, 80, 126, 127–28
rifles, 168, 184
Ritter, Captain, 36, 39; attack on
Boich, 88–92, 93, 95, 96, 97;
attack on Büllingen, 51–52,
53, 54, 55, 56; attack on
Hollerath, 69; attack on
Krinkelter Forest, 60, 65; in
Battle of the Bulge, 45, 46;
departure from unit, 106; in
Lechenich, 101; at Roer
River, 84
roads, corduroying, 83–84
Roer River, 75, 76–77, 84, 86–87

Roosevelt, Franklin, 165–66
Rose, Major General, 153
"Rose Pocket," 153
Ruethen, 153–61
runners, 157–58
Russian advance on Germany,
57–59
Russian physician, 187

Schuler, Captain, 106, 108; attack
on airfield, 132; attack on
Fernegierscheid, 141, 142,
143, 145, 146; attack on
Remagen bridgehead, 147;
attack on Ruethen, 154, 156;
en route to Steinbach, 152
Schwadorf, 108
Sechtem, 111
Seemosaye, 80–83
Seitz, Colonel, 32
self-inflicted wounds, 123
self-propelled gun, 63–64
Shealy, Captain, 20
Siegfried Line, 65–68
Sieg River, 136, 140
snipers, 154, 157
snow suits, 32
Spade, 79
Steinbach, 151–52

tanks, 39–40, 63, 90–91, 130–31,
137, 140, 170, 181–82; German, 101, 140, 144–45
3d Battalion of the 26th Infantry,
16, 58
time on target, 127
TOT (time on target), 127
trees as defensive weapons,
46–47, 178–79
trench foot, 34

Uckerath, 136, 137–38

variety show, 185–86
V-E day, 195–96

Verviers, 37–38
V-Is, 11, 24
Volk, Lieutenant, 113

Walbeberg, 106–8
weasels, 33
White, Lieutenant, 30–31, 33

white phosphorus rounds, 53–54,
   188
Windhausen, 164
Womack, Lieutenant, 58, 65, 89,
   93–94
wound, 93, 98
Wunnenberg, 153

ABOUT THE AUTHOR

Arthur Preston Price was born in Koblenz, Germany, where his father was a medical officer in the American Army of Occupation following World War I. He graduated from The Citadel in 1943, and his World War II experiences are chronicled in *The Last Kilometer*. Price's postwar career was in the field of strategic intelligence and included assignments in Czechoslovakia, Korea, and Germany. At one time an assistant professor of military science at The Citadel, he concluded his army service as chief of the studies division, Combat Development Command, at Fort Holabird, Maryland.

Colonel Price resides in El Paso, Texas, with his wife, Alice.